CHILD PROTECTION PRACTICES IN IRELAND

A Case Study

Helen Buckley

Caroline Skehill

Eoin O'Sullivan

Oak Tree Press

Dublin

Oak Tree Press
Merrion Building
Lower Merrion Street
Dublin 2, Ireland

A catalogue record of this book is
available from the British Library.

ISBN 1-86076-063-5

Printed in the Republic of Ireland by Colour Books Ltd.

CONTENTS

LIST OF FIGURES

LIST OF TABLES

ACKNOWLEDGMENTS

We would like to express our appreciation to a great many people without whose assistance this book would not have been possible. Martin Hynes, in his capacity as Programme Manager of the Community Care Programme in the South Eastern Health Board, commissioned the research on which this book is based, and offered us his support throughout the development of the study. Marie Kennedy, Child Care Development Officer with the Board was particularly helpful to us throughout the whole process and we would like to acknowledge her contribution. Our appreciation also goes to the social workers who completed the data sheets and allowed us access to their case records, and we are very grateful to the practitioners from the South Eastern Health Board and other agencies who gave us time from their busy work schedules to participate in interviews. A particular word of thanks is due to the parents who took part in the research. We would also like to convey appreciation to our colleagues in the Department of Social Studies, Trinity College for their support throughout the entire process.

Finally, for their assistance in the completion of this book, we are very grateful to Harry Ferguson and Anne O'Neill.

FOREWORD

Child protection and welfare has achieved an unprecedented position on the public agenda over the past decade, and the services set up to deal with it have been put under particular scrutiny. Policy development and new legislation have combined to bring about a more comprehensive, better resourced and more supported framework for child care practices. Yet, it needs to be acknowledged child protection is an uncertain and difficult area of work, which depends on a number of variables, not least of which is a sound knowledge base.

Section 11 of the Child Care Act 1991 empowers the health boards to undertake research into matters connected with the care and protection of children, and in 1995, the South Eastern Health Board commissioned the Department of Social Studies in Trinity College, Dublin, to carry out this study on child protection practices in the region. The key purpose in commissioning this review was to provide the South Eastern Health Board with independent, objective assessment of its child care services as an aid to management of the service and as a source of policy development. The research was carried out in late 1995 and early 1996, by Helen Buckley, Caroline Skehill and Eoin O'Sullivan. Our own staff were happy to participate in the study, and we are grateful for the co-operation of a number of other child care professionals and members of the Gardaí in the South East region, and particularly to those clients of our services who made a valuable contribution to the research.

The value of empirical research, carried out in the context of daily work, with its mundane as well as its extraordinary happenings, cannot be surpassed in terms of its ability to pinpoint areas where improvements need to be made as well as those in which progress has already been achieved. This is the first regional study of its kind to be completed in Ireland. We are pleased to make the findings available in published form, so that they may assist practitioners, policy makers, managers and students of child protection in raising their awareness regarding a broad range of professional issues. The South Eastern Health Board, in its training programme, has already implemented many of the recommendations made in the study, and is committed to continuous monitoring and improvement in the quality of its Child Care and Protection Services.

J.A. Cooney
Chief Executive Officer
South Eastern Health Board
September 1997

CHAPTER ONE

THE CHANGING NATURE OF CHILD WELFARE
SERVICES IN THE REPUBLIC OF IRELAND

INTRODUCTION

December 1996 marked a significant elaboration of the rapidly changing apparatus of child welfare services in Ireland. In that month, the final sections of the *Child Care Act, 1991* were enacted, thus fulfilling the promise, in the aftermath of the Kilkenny Incest Investigation (McGuinness, 1993), to have the Act fully implemented by the end of 1996. In the same month the long awaited *Children Bill* was published. The *Children Bill* aims to reform the system of juvenile justice in Ireland, together with the addition of a new section to the *Child Care Act, 1991,* which will give health boards the power to detain children in 'their best interests' (Maguire, 1996; O'Sullivan, 1996b). Thus, a structure is now in place which will formally replace the *Children Act, 1908* as the primary child welfare legislation in the country. Not only have the aforementioned legislative developments occurred, but, in addition, a range of other legislation has been enacted that has direct implications for the welfare of children in Ireland. These include the *Status of Children Act, 1987; Judicial Separation and Family Law Reform Act, 1989; Adoption Acts, 1988* and *1991; Child Abduction and Enforcement of Custody Act, 1991* and the *Adoptive Leave Act, 1995.*

Together with these developments, the Irish Government has ratified the United Nations Convention on the Rights of the Child and published its report to the Convention (1996). The Government has indicated that it is receptive to the development of an Ombudsperson for Children and the establishment of a National Council for Children. An Inspectorate of Child Care Services is also planned, and new legislation relating to school attendance is promised (Department of Education, 1994). The Department of Health published a discussion document on the mandatory reporting of all suspected child abuse in 1996. However, the eventual view of the Department of Health was that 'the introduction of mandatory reporting . . . in the immediate future would not be in the best interests of children' (Department of Health, 1996). Paralleling these legislative and policy events has been a series of unprecedented public revelations of abuse of young children by their families, by the clergy and by other persons in positions of trust. These revelations have shocked, confused and angered both the public and the polity, and have for the first time in the history of the State politicised child welfare. In turn, these revelations have placed enormous pressures on child welfare experts to respond to ever growing public expectations of protection and care for children suffering from, or facing, adversity in their lives.

This flurry of legislative and administrative action in the arena of child welfare over the past decade stands in marked contrast to the inertia in child welfare development since the foundation of the Irish State. Apart from a number of relatively minor amendments to the *Children Act, 1908* such as the *Children Act, 1941* and the *Children (Amendment) Acts* of 1949 and 1957, the system of child welfare inherited from the British administration remained largely intact until recently.

THE ORIGINS AND STRUCTURES OF CHILD WELFARE SERVICES IN IRELAND

From the foundation of the State in 1922 (and indeed prior to that period) the primary mode of dealing with the welfare and care needs of children was the placement of such children in residential care. Services for children, for whom alternatives to their lives on the street, or with their families, were deemed necessary, evolved gradually from the early 1820s. During this period a range of individuals and collections of individuals, motivated more often by sectarianism than by altruism, established orphanages to provide relief for the numerous 'street arabs' and 'hotentots' that inhabited the streets of Dublin in particular. In the 1840s, Catholic female religious orders or 'pious females' were particularly encouraged by Archbishop Cullen to establish homes for Catholic children who were roaming the streets, and at risk of proselytisation from Protestant evangelicals, who were also developing residential services for children in order to save them from unsavoury influences. By degrees, a number of private orphanages were established under the patronage of either the Catholic or Protestant Churches (see Robins, 1980; Barnes, 1989, for further details).

Residential establishments for children who were either orphaned, abandoned or rejected were seen as sites where these children from the 'dangerous and perishing classes' could be trained, albeit within the limits of their subordinate station, to become useful and productive members of society. In addition to making these children productive cogs in the economic, social and military machinery of the 19th century social order, 'all philanthropists, whether Catholic or Protestant, were intent on imparting their own religious views to their charges, and amassing souls for God was seen as part of their duty' (Luddy, 1995: 83). It was also argued that many of these children, if not rescued by these charitable child-savers, were at risk of imprisonment, as criminal law at that time did not differentiate between children and adults in terms of the sentences received, and the form of punishment delivered (Barnes, 1989). Furthermore there was a growing awareness of the inappropriateness of workhouses for the development of children as witnessed through the high rates of mortality therein (Hancock, 1859). Concern regarding these children was translated into a flurry of legislative activity which moulded the structure of a child welfare apparatus that proved resilient well into the next century.

Reformatory Schools

Firstly, as a result of pressure from a number of sources, and after much debate regarding denominational control over such institutions, reformatory schools were established in Ireland under the *Reformatory School (Ireland) Act, 1858*. The legislation allowed for voluntary agencies to establish reformatory schools and to be certified for State aid. However, State aid was only available for the *maintenance* of those children committed to the schools and not for *capital* costs. Within a short period, voluntary committees were established to take advantage of the new legislation and by 1870, ten reformatory schools had been established and certified in Ireland, and the seven of these which catered for members of the Catholic faith were run and managed by religious orders. The overt objective of the reformatory schools was the provision of a humane alternative to adult prisons for children who were deemed to have broken the law, and to attempt to reform their characters through a programme of training and education.

Boarding-out Children

Secondly, there was concern regarding the sanitary and moral environment of children growing up in the workhouses which had been established under the *Poor Relief (Ireland) Act, 1838*. In 1862, the *Poor Relief (Ireland) Act,* under section 9, stated:

> . . . and whereas it has been found that the mortality among infant children admitted into workhouses without their mothers is very large, and that in other respects the workhouses are not well suited in all cases for the care and nurture of such children during infancy, and it is, therefore, expedient to extend the powers of Boards of Guardians for the relief of destitute poor children who are orphans or who have been deserted by their parents, it shall be lawful for the Board of Guardians to provide for the relief of any orphan or deserted child out of the workhouse if they shall think fit to do so by placing such child out at nurse according to their discretion.

This put in place the system of fostering, or boarding-out children in Ireland, which, with occasional minor adjustments, was to form the basis for a system of fostering for the next century.

Industrial Schools

The *third* key legislative development in the establishment of services for children was the passing of the *Industrial Schools Act* in 1868. Like the system of reformatory schools, industrial schools were based on models already in existence in Scotland and England and were imported into the Irish system to provide a service to those children who had not committed offences, but who, due to their uncontrolled lifestyles, were at risk of committing criminal offences. However, in certain cases, industrial schools also accepted young offenders and this was reaffirmed under Section 58(3) of the *Children Act, 1908*. Many of the existing orphanages readily converted into industrial schools, while others were newly constructed and were thus regulated and inspected on a regular basis. In return they received a capitation grant for each child committed to the Industrial school. A number of orphanages, however, decided to remain outside the statutory system of regulation, and to continue to operate on a purely voluntary basis, funded entirely by donations.

The Children Act, 1908

The primary legislation governing Irish child care services for much of the 20th century was the *Children Act, 1908*. This Act consolidated the mass of legislation which had regulated the treatment and provision of services for children since the middle of the 19th century. The Act was to remain in place with only minor amendments until the gradual implementation of the *Child Care Act, 1991*, despite a recognition by the Department of Education that the 1908 Act 'was drafted without reference to the circumstances peculiar to Ireland' (Department of Education, 1926: 87).

The numbers of children in institutional care remained exceedingly high for the first half of the 20th century, averaging between 7,000 and 8,000 at any one time, and it was only from the early 1950s that their numbers declined significantly. Since the early 1970s, the numbers of children in institutional care has declined further, and of the 3,588 children in the care of the health boards at the end of 1995, only 585 or 16 per cent were in residential care, compared to 3,003 children in foster care. However, in recent years, the long-term decline in the number of children entering substitute care has been reversed, as highlighted in Figure 1.1. The number of children entering substitute care has risen from 2,840 in 1990 to 3,588 in 1995, an increase of 26.3 per cent.

FIGURE 1.1: NUMBER OF CHILDREN IN FOSTER CARE AND
RESIDENTIAL CARE, 1965–1995

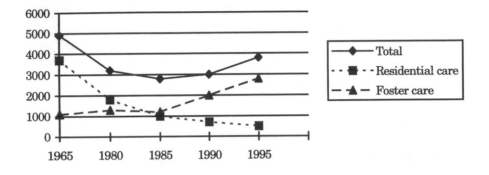

CHILD WELFARE AND CHANGING PARADIGMS OF INTERVENTION

The 1937 Constitution's ascription of the 'inalienable and imperscriptable rights' of parents had an effect on the development of all policy and practice in relation to state intervention with children and their families. The family was recognised as the 'primary and fundamental unit group of society' (Article 42 of the Irish Constitution). For many years following the establishment of the Irish Constitution, the Catholic Church exerted strong control over the extent of state involvement into what it considered the private domain of family life.[1] Breen *et al.* (1990) suggest that, up to the 1960s, a distinctive combination of religious orthodoxy, family based production, and the Catholic Church's unrivalled prestige and legitimacy left the family largely outside the sphere of State intervention. Paradoxically, this embracing of the family as a fundamental unit in society was not matched by a parallel effort to enhance the welfare of children. Fahey has argued that since the 1960s a greater concern for the personal rights and needs of children has emerged. This has involved:

---

[1] Fahey, however, has suggested that an exception to this rule was the enforcement of school attendance legislation and that 'it is possible to see that school attendance enforcement introduced a regulation of families that was unprecedented both in its scale of application and in the intrusive, coercive manner in which it affected families' (1992: 38).

... [a] de-emphasis on subordination, silence and service to adults in cultural definitions of children's place in life. It has led to a growing disapproval for the use of physical beatings, intimidation, ridicule, fear and shaming as devices for disciplining children — in short, to a rejection of many of the standard child-rearing devices routinely used in the past, both by parents and others who were in authority over children (NESC, 1996: 44).

In addition to the broader cultural and social changes sweeping Irish society from the 1960s, there was a fundamental critique of the role of the institutional child care provisions generated by the publication of three key reports in the second half of that decade. These were the Tuairim report 'Some of our Children' in 1966; the publication of *Investment in Education* by the OECD in the same year and the publication of the *Committee of Inquiry into Industrial and Reformatory Schools* in 1970. These reports highlighted the inadequacy of the *Children Act, 1908* in meeting the needs of children, the undesirability of widespread use of institutional care for children and the lack of State involvement in the provision of child care services more generally. However, of equal importance was the changing role of the Catholic Church in Ireland. All of the industrial schools in Ireland since the foundation of the State, as well as the majority of orphanages, were run by Catholic religious orders. The impact of Vatican Two was to exert an enormous change on the role that the Catholic Church saw for itself in contemporary Ireland, so in fact, by the mid-1960s, many of the changes recommended by the three aforementioned reports had already been put in train by the religious orders themselves. The closure of 14 industrial schools between 1964 and 1969, at the request of the religious orders themselves, and the movement away from large institutions towards smaller units, were a result of some of the changes convulsing the Catholic Church at that time. The key importance of the reports on residential care was the formulation of a strategy that was to start to push the State centre stage in the delivery and organisation of residential care in Ireland. The period immediately following the publication of the *Report on Industrial Schools and Reformatories* (The Kennedy Report) saw the term 'industrial and reformatory schools' replaced by the terms 'groups homes' and 'special schools' in day to day usage (although not legally). More importantly, with the establishment of health boards in 1970, the Department of Education itself was becoming a minor player in the care of deprived children. The numbers of social workers working in community care were increasing, and replacing the former agents of referrals to residential care, such as the ISPCC (Irish Society for the Prevention of Cruelty to Children). A *Task Force on Child Care Services* which was established in 1974, and which eventually published its final report in 1980, commented that:

> . . . the most striking feature of the child care scene in Ireland was the alarming complacency and indifference of both the general public and various government departments and statutory bodies responsible for the welfare of children. This state of affairs illustrated clearly the use by a society of residential establishments to divest itself of responsibility for deprived children and delinquent children (1980: 182).

The Department of Health was given a central role in child care services in 1974. However, it was not until 1984 that full responsibility for industrial schools was transferred from the Department of Education to the Department of Health, which already had responsibility for a number of voluntary homes approved for funding by the Minister for Health. The Department of Education continues to be responsible for the remaining reformatory schools, a number of industrial schools which accept young offenders and an assessment centre. (Under the provisions of the Children Bill, 1996, these centres will be re-titled Children Detention Schools.)

It was only from the late 1960s that a 'social risk' model of child care which had influenced policy for the previous hundred years became displaced by a more developmental model of child care, brought about by the discovery of the 'deprived child' in Ireland. Prior to this period child care intervention was viewed as 'a means of social control rather than of individual fulfilment' (O'Sullivan, 1979: 211). The primary facets of the emerging developmental model were a disenchantment with institutionalisation and the need to move beyond a narrow interpretation of child care. Rather than focusing, almost exclusively, on the *physical* needs of the child, the need to incorporate *emotional* and *psychological* dimensions in promoting the welfare of children gained acceptance.

The Kennedy Report, prefaced with the statement that 'All children need love, care and security if they are to develop into full and mature adults' (1970: v), most clearly articulated this shift. The recommendations of the Kennedy Report were taken up by a range of child care agencies and in particular the Campaign for the Care of the Deprived Child (CARE, 1972). The hosting of a conference on child care in 1971 (Council for Social Welfare) and the publication of the CARE Memorandum in 1972 added momentum to the reform that had been initiated by the Tuairim report on residential child care in 1966. O'Sullivan has argued that:

> . . . [the] application of changing interpretations of equality to the life circumstances of children who came into care, mediated to the public through conferences, publications and considerable media coverage, was to be one of the major sources of the 'discovery' of the deprived child in Ireland (1979: 215).

Thus, the discourse of the 'depraved' child, which shaped the application of intervention of the State and those to whom it delegated child care responsibilities, was to shift to a discourse that placed a premium on the notion of deprivation. This trend was to find further elaboration in the report of the Task Force on Child Care Services. The Task Force was established in 1974 to

> . . . make recommendations on the extension of services for deprived children and children at risk, to prepare a Bill updating the law in relation to children and to make recommendations on whatever administrative reforms it considered necessary in the child care services (1980: 1).

The report, which was eventually published in 1980, was the clearest official pronunciation on the dramatic shift that had occurred over the previous 15 years. There was considerable disagreement between members of the Task Force on key areas, such as juvenile justice and children, and the Constitution, necessitating a supplementary report. Although a considerable time-lag existed between the publication of the report and subsequent administrative and legislative change, it nevertheless represented the embodiment of many of the ideals of the reformers of the late 1960s and early 1970s and gave full expression to the developmental model of child welfare. The publication of the Task Force report gradually set in train a series of legislative developments which were to gradually repeal the *Children Act, 1908*.

THE CHANGING ROLE OF THE STATE IN CHILD WELFARE SERVICES

Alongside these long-term shifts in the nature of child welfare provision in Ireland, has been a critique of the role of the State in the provision of child welfare services. In interpreting recent changes in the evolution of child welfare services in Ireland, we need to be mindful that the role of the State in the direct provision of services has, until recently, been marginal. It was only with the establishment of health boards in 1970, as a result of the *Health Act, 1970*, that the State began to play a key role in the provision of child care services. The Act established eight regional health boards, each of which incorporated a number of community care areas. Prior to this Act, services were delivered by local authorities who had a multitude of tasks, of which services for children formed only a very minor proportion.

Health boards have responsibility for three main programmes: (1) community care services; (2) general hospital services; and (3) special hospital services. Community care services are further subdivided into three sub-programmes: (i) Community protection sub-programme; (ii) Community health services sub-programme; and (iii) Community welfare sub-programme. Services for children are provided through the community welfare sub-programme of community care services (NESC, 1987). Social workers employed directly by the health boards have primary responsibility for the provision of child welfare services, and their numbers have grown substantially since the 1970s. However, the role of social workers in the structure of community care has given rise to some dissatisfaction. As Butler has argued:

> While social workers are employed directly by health boards, they have persistently expressed dissatisfaction with an administrative arrangement in which top-level decision-making in what they perceive to be their professional domain remains the prerogative of the Director of Community care, a public health medicine official. During the 1980s there was a protracted but ultimately unsuccessful campaign by social workers to establish a separate administrative programme; this was aimed at distinguishing personal social services from community health services, thereby granting social workers a degree of professional autonomy which they had not previously enjoyed (1996: 303).

Prior to the 1970s, virtually all residential services were managed by voluntary agencies, and the local authorities and the ISPCC had responsibility for the needs of children not placed in institutional care. Although two Inspectors of Boarded-out Children were established in 1904, and a number of children's officers appointed in 1959 as a consequence of the passing of the *Children (Amendment) Act, 1957*, the role of state agencies in the direct provision of welfare services for children was limited. In 1974 there was a total of only 235 social workers employed nationally, distributed between health boards, local authorities and voluntary agencies. By 1993 there were 726 social workers employed nationally, with 499 employed directly by health boards. Since 1993, over 900 new posts have been created for the child care services.

Although many of these developments precede the extraordinary series of events of the early 1990s, it is clear that the radical changes currently occurring in the organisation and nature of child welfare services in Ireland owe much to the heightened public awareness of child abuse in particular, and that these events have shaped the provision of child welfare services in a specific manner.

CHILD ABUSE AND CHILD PROTECTION IN IRELAND

It is only within the past decade that child abuse has achieved a significant position on the social and political agenda in Ireland, due in no small way to the unprecedented publicity given to high-profile cases. Revelations of sexual abuse of young children by their families, by the clergy and by other persons in positions of trust, together with recent disclosures about physical abuse of children in residential care settings, have combined critical attention on both the existence of child abuse as a serious problem in Ireland, and on the system which deals with it. It may be argued that if the period up to the 1970s was characterised by a concern with the 'depraved child' and the 1970s and 1980s with the 'deprived child', we have now entered into an era where the focus of intervention is concerned with the 'abused child'.

The evolution of the child protection system in Ireland was heavily influenced by international trends and events as well as by Ireland's own unique social framework. The 'rediscovery' of child abuse in the 1960s in Britain and the USA with the work of Kempe and Helfer (1968), and the repercussions in Britain of the first child abuse 'scandals' started to have an influence on awareness of the problem in Ireland. The ISPCC, using its links in Britain, acted as a conduit through which these matters were brought to public as well as professional attention. In 1975, the Department of Health set up a committee to discuss the issue of 'non-accidental injury to children'. This heavily medically dominated committee agreed that there was a significant problem of non-accidental injury to children in Ireland, and recommended an examination of the position and the suggestion of procedures for dealing with such cases and ensuring the co-operation of parties dealing with it.

The public awareness of child abuse as a social problem in Ireland in the early 1970s is illustrated by an early piece of research which was carried out by Smith and Deasy (1977) in Our Lady's Hospital for Sick Children, in Dublin. Their findings suggested that, between 1971 and 1976, child abuse accounted for one in seven hundred admissions to their hospital. They forecast that increased awareness and recognition of the problem would at least double this incidence. In fact, statistics collected by the Department of Health ten years later, in 1983–87, revealed that the number of confirmed cases now being recognised had not simply doubled, it had increased by 500 per cent (Gilligan, 1991).

The first report of the *Committee on Non-Accidental Injury* was published in 1976, and this represented the basis for all subsequent guidelines issued by the Department of Health. Early reactions to this report by organisations such as the Irish Association of Social Workers were critical of its over-concentration on the detection of physical signs of child maltreatment, and its neglect of the emotional, psychological and social dimensions of child abuse. There was also criticism both of the emphasis on detection at the expense of longer term management, and the absence of plans to develop prevention and intervention skills. The first edition of national child abuse guidelines was published in 1977, known as the *Memorandum on Non-Accidental Injury to Children*. A later edition was published in 1980, followed by another revised version in 1983. The 1983 guidelines had been preceded by the first investigation into child abuse in Ireland. This had been a rather low-key examination of the deaths of two children who were on social workers' caseloads. The investigation identified a lack of cohesion, poor communication and lack of co-ordination in the child protection services. At the same time, however, the report acknowledged the inadequacies of the system. The 1983 guidelines again concentrated mainly on physical abuse, but included 'injury resulting from sexual abuse' in the definitions of child abuse offered.

The number of reported cases of child sexual abuse increased dramatically during the mid-1980s, accompanied by the beginnings of considerable media attention on the issue. McKeown and Gilligan (1991) trace the first indication of professional concern with this problem in Ireland to a multi-disciplinary seminar on incest, organised by the Irish Association of Social Workers in 1983; an outcome of this meeting was a recognition of the need for an Irish study on child sexual abuse. In 1984, the Irish Council for Civil Liberties set up a Working Party on Child Sexual Abuse, whose brief was 'to gather data, to review existing policies, services and laws concerning child sexual abuse and to make specific recommendations' (Cooney & Torode, 1989). *The Report of the Working Party* was informed by a number of research studies specially commissioned, a review of recent studies and statistics, and consultation visits to other countries. The working party was aware that child sexual abuse was 'defined differently in different cultures and contexts in ways which either lack precision or applicability' (1989: 2) and sought to explore the problem in an Irish context, taking account of features specific to it, which impacted on the way the problem was understood and addressed. The studies which were commissioned by the working party were themselves affected by the fact that, in 1984, the existence of child sexual abuse was barely recognised in Ireland, and there was no ready access to victims, which obviously limited the researchers.

Factors which, in the view of the ICCL Working Party, acted as constraints to effective action included insufficient support for voluntary and self-help groups, and their lack of integration with professional services; lack of information and training on the subject; and the assumption in official guidance that child sexual abuse could be dealt with adequately in the same fashion as non-accidental injury. The report also criticised the *ad hoc* fashion in which funding was contracted to voluntary bodies to provide services, without specification of the type or quality of work expected. This, they considered, led at times to divergence in standards and poor co-ordination. The lack of a knowledge base which could usefully be applied in an Irish context was particularly noted by the working party, who felt that the need to rely on international research findings ignored some of the contextual realities and particular demographic factors which needed to be considered in relation to Irish children who may be at risk of sexual abuse.

Many of the reforms which were advocated by the ICCL Working Party were also recommended in the Law Reform Commission *Report on Child Sexual Abuse* (1990). The Law Reform Commission introduced, for the first time in Irish policy or guidance about child protection, the stipulation that the Gardaí should be involved in the 'early stages' of investigation of child sexual abuse, in order to facilitate the possibility of a prosecution. In a similar legalistic vein, they strongly recommended the empowerment of the health boards to seek *ex parte* barring orders in order to remove abusers from the home (which finally came to fruition in the *Domestic Violence Act, 1996*). In keeping with these reforms, the Law Reform Commission suggested a re-vamping of the court system to render it more 'child-friendly', the introduction of a special panel of suitable solicitors; and the availability of special information and training to the judiciary.

These important documents reflect the growing awareness of child sexual abuse in Ireland in the 1980s, which had its origins in the way that the problem was being re-framed internationally. Changing concepts of child sexual abuse (CSA) depended for their acceptance and expansion on the work of voluntary associations and pressure groups, such as the Irish Association of Social Workers, the Incest Crisis Service and the Rape Crisis Centre. In the late 1980s, the Department of Health signalled its acknowledgement of the problem by allocating funds for research and for the establishment of services (McKeown & Gilligan, 1991).

In 1987, the Department of Health published guidelines (*Child Abuse Guidelines*) which gave a comprehensive definition of abuse as: 'physical injuries, severe neglect and sexual or emotional abuse'. The Guide abandoned for the first time the concept of child abuse as consisting exclusively of 'non-accidental injury'. The importance of inter-agency and inter-professional work was emphasised, and the centrality of case conferences underlined. For the first time, the roles and responsibilities of all professionals in the child protection network were outlined. The primary statutory response to growing concerns regarding the unmet needs and welfare of children in Ireland and the limitations of the *Children Act, 1908* in addressing these needs was the enactment of the *Child Care Act, 1991*.

THE CHILD CARE ACT, 1991

The Child Care Act, 1991 represents the culmination of attempts to provide a modern legislative framework to deal with children who are neglected or at risk in Ireland. Existing legislation, primarily in the form of the *Children Act 1908*, was deemed inadequate in catering for the needs of children at risk in Irish society. The 1908 Act represented the changing recognition of childhood that had evolved since the mid-nineteenth century. The 1991 Act incorporated, modified and repealed much of the existing legislation in relation to children under its broad remit, thus becoming the first legislation to deal with children in a comprehensive manner.

The *Building on Reality* document produced by the Fine Gael/Labour Party Coalition Government in 1985, stated an intention to introduce three Bills in relation to the care and protection of children. The original intention of the Government was to produce a single comprehensive Children's Bill which would deal with all aspects of the law, including the care and protection of children, adoption and juvenile justice. However, this was viewed as posing substantial Constitutional problems and instead it was decided to introduce a series of bills dealing with the issues in turn. The first bill, the *Children (Care and Protection) Bill*, was designed to update and extend the law relating to the care and protection of children. The composition of the Act was in many senses non-partisan, based on a high degree of consensus by both politicians and interest groups involved in child care, although with some disputes regarding the details. In light of the body of evidence presented regarding the need for new child care legislation, the slow rate of progress in producing new legislation is perplexing. As O'Connor has observed:

> One of the puzzling enigmas of Irish Social Policy is the contrast between, on the one hand, the clear endorsement of the family as the pivotal unit in Irish Society and, on the other hand, the reluctance up to very recently to initiate legislative reform to protect the most vulnerable members of that group — children (O'Connor, 1992: 215).

However, despite a broad consensus with regard to the thrust of the Act, many of its elements have given rise to difficulties and disagreements in implementation, and certain litigation has occurred in order to clarify the operation of some of its sections. This is primarily because of the enabling nature of much of the Act and the vagueness of many of its powers. The slow progress of the Act through the Oireachtas was mirrored by the rate of implementation, or as Gilligan describes it, its 'genteel pace of reform' (1992–93: 366). Originally proposed to be fully implemented by the end of 1998, the Kilkenny Incest Inquiry (McGuinness, 1993) and other allegations of abuse against children, accelerated its rate of implementation. Although it was formally enacted on the 10th of

July 1991, it came into force on a phased basis, and was only fully implemented in December 1996.

Purpose and Provisions of the Child Care Act, 1991

The purpose of the Act is to 'up-date the law in relation to the care of children who have been assaulted, ill-treated, neglected or sexually abused or who are at risk' (Explanatory Memorandum accompanying the publication of the Act: 1). The promotion of the welfare of children is seen as the paramount principle underpinning the Act. This implies a shift from a reactive deployment of resources to a more proactive approach which aims to involve parents, children and carers and a desire to facilitate inter-agency collaboration although, in practice, a reactive model largely operates.

The main provisions of the Act are

- The placing of a statutory duty on Health Boards to promote the welfare of children who are not receiving adequate care and protection up to the age of 18

- The strengthening of the powers of the Health Boards to provide child care and family support services

- The improvement of the procedures to facilitate immediate intervention by Health Boards and the Gardaí where children are in danger

- The revision of provisions to enable the courts to place children who have been assaulted, ill-treated, neglected or sexually abused or who are at risk, in the care of or under the supervision of regional Health Boards

- The introduction of arrangements for the supervision and inspection of pre-school services, and

- The revision of provisions in relation to the registration and inspection of residential centres for children.

Thus, in a remarkably short period of time, the legislative framework for dealing with children in need of care has changed dramatically. The *Child Care Act, 1991*, for the first time, clarifies the role, duties and powers of the health boards. In addition to specifying the health boards' obligations to protect children in emergencies, and provide and review satisfactory arrangements for those who are admitted to 'care', the Act sanctions health boards 'to promote the welfare of children in its area'. Essentially, the underlying philosophy of the Act is pro-active, and the health boards are required to 'have regard to the principle that it is generally in the best interests of a child to be brought up in his or her own family'. In common with British legislation, the Act reflects the 'competing discourses' of treatment and punishment (Merrick, 1996), and essentially expects practitioners to walk the delicate tightrope between giving primacy to the protection of children and minimising State intervention into family life. New procedures and guidelines for the implementation of the Act are placing increasing demands on social workers and other professionals working with children, and there may be a time lag between the enactment of various sections of the Act and their full implementation. In order to meet the increasing demands on the social work service with the implementation of the Act, there has been a significant increase in social work personnel with the introduction of Team Leader posts in each of the Community Care areas. Additionally, a number of Community Care child care workers have been employed, and a number of services have been developed for assessment, treatment and family support work in order to both respond to the needs of victims of child abuse, and to address primary and secondary prevention.

CURRENT ISSUES IN CHILD WELFARE AND PROTECTION IN IRELAND

Despite the broad *child welfare* thrust of the *Child Care Act, 1991*, in practice, much of the time and energy of those charged with promoting the welfare of children has been directed into a more narrowly focused *child protection* framework. This has largely come about as a consequence of a series of unprecedented inquiries into allegations of child abuse, both within families of origin and in substitute care. This situation is not unique to Ireland. As Parton has pointed out in relation to the Children Act, 1989 in Britain:

> Not only are the family support aspirations and sections of
> the Act being implemented partially and not prioritised, but
> the child protection system is overloaded and not coping
> with the increased demands made of it (1997: 3).

Perhaps the most significant investigation was the *Report of The
Kilkenny Incest Investigation*. This investigation concerned the
sexual and physical abuse of a young woman by her father over
many years. The notoriety surrounding the case arose out of media reports of the father's trial and sentencing for incest. It became known that the health and social services had had over one
hundred contacts with the family in the thirteen years prior to
the prosecution, during which time the abuse had continued. The
television coverage of the case included an interview with the
young woman, known by the pseudonym of 'Mary', in which she
criticised the social worker involved. In the wake of further widespread condemnation of the child care services, the Minister for
Health announced a public inquiry. The inquiry team, under the
chairpersonship of a Judge, Catherine McGuinness, reported after
three months. The report identified a number of deficiencies in
both the child protection system, and in the professional activities
of the various practitioners involved, particularly in relation to
poor inter-agency co-operation, weaknesses in management and
'lack of the necessary effective probing' (1993: 88). However, like
several British inquiries (London Borough of Brent, 1985 (The
Beckford Report); Butler Sloss, 1988 (The Cleveland Inquiry)) the
investigating team went beyond their original brief to comment
on the 'ambivalence of the community as a whole to this type of
violence' (1993: 89). They also acknowledged the complexity involved in determining the boundaries between personal autonomy
and State intervention, the preservation of the balance between
the rights of individual and family privacy and 'the duty of the
State or society to intervene in situations of moral danger or
abuse'. While the report made very specific recommendations for
improvements in the child protection system, the inquiry team
acknowledged that:

> Procedures in themselves, whether statutory or otherwise,
> are not a substitute for good practice, and services must be

responsive to local circumstances and resources must be available to ensure that intervention is effective (1993: 97).

The recommendations of the *Report of the Kilkenny Incest Investigation* were broad in their attempts to address the issue of child abuse, but they were limited to the extent that they emanated from a retrospective study of the events surrounding one case. Child abuse inquiries, while valuable in themselves, may ignore the contextual realities in which child protection practice is situated, and it is questionable whether or not an inquiry provides a suitable theoretical foundation for the design of a set of general principles aimed at governing professional practice (see Buckley, 1996a). However, child protection policy making in Ireland has tended to follow high profile happenings in a political, piecemeal fashion (McGrath, 1996), and the *Report of the Kilkenny Incest Investigation* provided the catalyst needed to progress the child care services, at that time.

The effect of the investigation was to place the issue of child abuse firmly in the public and political arena for perhaps the first time in the history of the Irish State.[2] It also marked the start of a series of inquiries and allegations of child abuse and neglect that shocked and confused both the public and the polity. The role of the Catholic Church in the provision of child care services, and the apparent concealment of members of the Church who had abused children over long periods of time, resulted in unprecedented public anger regarding their role. Allegations regarding cruelty to children in child care institutions run by the Catholic Church focused on the control the Church had in such institutions and the residual role of the State. In early 1996 a further two official investigations into child abuse and neglect were published

---

[2] Prior to the *Report of the Kilkenny Incest Investigation*, only two official investigations into the abuse or death of children in the care of the State were conducted. One was the narrowly focused report into the death of 35 children in St. Joseph's Orphanage in Cavan in 1943 (*Report of the Tribunal of Inquiry into the Fire at St. Joseph's Orphanage, Main Street, Cavan, 1943*). The report concentrated solely on the causes of the fire that caused the death of the children. The second was a short press statement released by the Minister for Health regarding the circumstances in which two children in the protective care of the Eastern Health Board died in 1982 (Government Information Services, 1982).

after long delays due to concerns around libelling of individuals involved. The report into the death of Kelly Fitzgerald (entitled *Kelly: A Child is Dead*, 1996) and the report into allegations of abuse in the largest children's home in the country, Madonna House, heightened public awareness of the vulnerability of children and the apparent inability of statutory services to prevent the abuse.

Child Abuse Guidelines in Ireland

One of the inevitable consequences of the Kilkenny case, and the other child abuse scandals which followed, has been the tightening up of procedural guidance for child protection practitioners. These relate to a number of professions. The role of schools in the identification, investigation and management of child abuse was emphasised in the *Report of the Kilkenny Incest Investigation*, which firmly endorsed the implementation of the child abuse guidelines for teachers which had been in operation since the early 1990s.[3] The Kilkenny report had also drawn attention to the need for a smooth flow of information between the police and the health boards, and recommended the introduction of an agreed policy for effective inter-agency communication. Work which had already been in progress between the Departments of Health and Justice culminated in the publication in April 1995 of a set of procedures outlining the necessary steps in joint notification of child abuse between the Irish police force — the Gardaí — and the health boards.[4]

The effectiveness of these guidelines is debatable and continues to raise doubts about the feasibility of imposing technical solutions to an area as complex as child abuse. For example, a study in the North West of Ireland on the role of teachers in child abuse (Kelly, 1996) indicates that there is a high level of ambiguity about the following of procedures, and that teachers process their concerns about child abuse in different ways, not all within the

---

[3] *Procedures for Dealing with Allegations or Suspicions of Child Abuse.* Department of Education, 1991.

[4] *Notification of Suspected Cases of Child Abuse between the Gardaí and the Health Boards.* Department of Health, 1995.

official system. This ambiguity is seen to stem from a 'less than clear societal mandate to carry out their caring role towards children' (1996: 84).

The usefulness of the Department of Health's 1995 guidelines for the *Notification of Suspected Child Abuse between the Health Boards and the Gardaí* has been questioned (Buckley, 1996), given the hurried manner in which they became operational. The implementation of these procedures represented a move towards the improvement of inter-agency co-operation, but were introduced without preparatory training and without any structural arrangements to facilitate the joint work which they prescribed. Research on Garda/social work relations in Ireland (Buckley, 1993) had highlighted many of the reasons for poor co-operation between the two agencies. Principal among these were the lack of any arrangements for communication; there were no designated Gardaí to deal with cases of child abuse, record-keeping was poor, and differing shift patterns caused delays in contact. A reluctance to co-operate emanated from the stereotypical images each agency had of the other; the social workers perceived the Gardaí as 'insensitive', 'poorly educated', and having 'chips on their shoulders', while the Gardaí saw the social workers as 'do-gooders', 'useless', 'anti-police' and 'over the top about confidentiality'. Research carried out since the implementation of the procedures indicates that many of the previously identified problems remain. While there is evidence that, in the UK, relationships between social workers and police have considerably improved within a context of specialisation and training (Hallett, 1995) there is no indication of any commitment to build a similar infra-structure in Ireland. For Ferguson, in his analysis of the events that have brought the issue of child care to public attention,

> . . . these extraordinary social changes have also contributed to a trajectory where, within the expert system, child care and protection is being pushed more and more in the direction of a bureaucratic, investigative approach to working with children and families (1996: 30).

As a consequence of these pressures, children whose welfare needs cannot be encapsulated within a specific child protection framework are increasingly unlikely to receive adequate services from the statutory authorities, although their welfare needs may be defined in the *Child Care Act, 1991*. Child welfare has increasingly become identified with child sexual abuse. Over the past decade, increasing recognition of the problem of child abuse, particularly child sexual abuse, has resulted in the child welfare services delivered by the health boards being increasingly channelled into this arena of child welfare. On both a national and a regional level, there is a significant increase in the number of child abuse and neglect referrals to the Health Boards in general. Nationally, the number of child abuse notifications rose from 434 in 1983 to 6,415 in 1995. Reports of child sexual abuse rose from 37 in 1983 to 2,441 in 1995 as shown in Figure 1.2.

FIGURE 1.2: REPORTS OF CHILD ABUSE AND CHILD SEXUAL ABUSE, 1983–1995

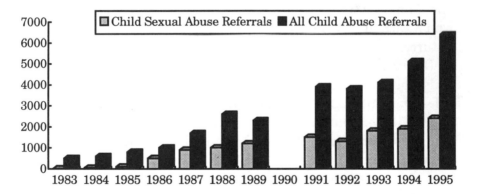

Policy in relation to child protection in Ireland observes a certain rhetoric, and contains assumptions about the wisdom and efficacy of following a particular line. On the one hand, child protection practice to date has escaped the bureaucratic and cumbersome requirements imposed in some European countries, but at the same time, in many ways, policy makers have failed to take due account of the position faced on a daily basis by practitioners at the front-line. It has already been pointed out that new initiatives in child protection policy have tended to be politically driven, rather than emerging from the recommendations of empirical research, and there is strong evidence that, in the process, they may lack a certain amount of realism and applicability.

Recent Messages from Research in Britain

Given the lack of published empirical research in the Irish context until relatively recently, and the fact that policy and practice in Ireland owes much to international influences, particularly from Britain, a brief review of recent research in Britain highlights the similarities and dissimilarities with the Irish situation and provides a number of the research issues that will examined in this book. In the 1980s, while child protection and welfare policies in Britain were significantly influenced by the numerous child abuse inquiries which were published during that decade (Parton, 1991), several studies sought to examine the 'real-life', or day to day, practice of child protection workers, mainly social workers, in local authorities. Most notable were the works of Dingwall, Eekelaar and Murray (1983), Corby (1987) and Pithouse (1987), each of whom carried out empirical, longitudinal studies of a qualitative nature.

Dingwall *et al.* sought to examine the social construction of child abuse. They hypothesised that the complex process of identification, confirmation and disposal actually produced abuse and neglect rather than something which was inherent in the child's presenting condition. Their study focused on decision making procedures, and they sought to refute the view that child abuse and neglect are obvious to the trained eye. Dingwall *et al.* identified two types of evidence that may prompt agency staff to define a particular child as abused or neglected. The first of these is *clinical* evidence, that is, physical data. The second is *social* evidence, data which are thrown up by an investigation of the child's environment, quality of relationship with parents, material conditions, and circumstances of the injury. However, the authors were impressed by what they considered to be a significant anomaly between reported child abuse incidents, and those which they felt should be statistically present if 'operational rules' were applied, i.e. if everything that could be regarded as abusive behaviour on the part of parents was recorded as such. What they found was a 'rarity of allegations of mistreatment'. They sought to explain why most possible 'candidates' for the child protection system were eliminated, and found their answer in what they identified as an additional assessment of parents' moral character, calling it 'the rule of optimism'. According to this rule, child protection workers are 'required' to think the best of parents. Dingwall *et al.* defined this rule, not as an individual psychological failing of the practitioner involved in investigation, but as the practical reflection of a liberal philosophy, which has its origins in the evolution of a liberal society where the family was seen as an important check on State power.

Decision making and adherence to agency guidelines were addressed by Pithouse (1987). He found that case categories and formal procedures have limited relevance for the way in which work is carried out, and do not indicate the amount, style or quality of work that is applied. The reason given was that the multiplicity of events and contingencies in child care cases bears no relation to the abstract generality of broad directives. Social workers were impelled to rely on their own experience, which is corroborated with close colleagues, resulting in increasing in-group dependence and loyalty to local views of practice.

Corby (1987), like Pithouse, found that while there was a clear cut guide to the investigation of child abuse, social workers found it hard in practice to adhere to these procedures, as the guidelines leave many problematic practical and ethical questions unanswered. In Pithouse's study, the prevailing philosophy behind the lack of adherence to procedures was that it was only front line social workers who were 'doing the job' who could manage the unpredictable work world, and who evolve their practice out of a shared occupational experience. In Corby's study, however, lack of adherence to guidelines had more to do with the social workers' unease at carrying out an investigative role. Corby confirmed Dingwall *et al.*'s finding that front line workers tended not to bring cases into the open unless forced to do so by the fact that other agencies became involved. He found that an informal screening of cases operated. In particular, those cases where social workers were already involved tended not to be processed through the child abuse system. Corby considered that the reason for this was that such action might lead to an over-reaction to families' problems, and to social workers losing control of situations which they felt most suited to deal with.

Corby's research went further than the two other studies mentioned, to examine the ongoing decision making, review and management of child protection cases. He found that the unease which social workers felt about the authoritarian role they were expected to carry out became more explicit when they were 'monitoring' cases in the longer term. The research argued that, in social work with families where child abuse is suspected or alleged, workers find it very difficult to combine the roles of care and control. The consequence was that there was considerable variety in the ways of monitoring child abuse cases where children remained in their own homes. Corby found that the preference of the social workers for a helping or supporting role lead to a confused and confusing form of monitoring.

The above studies, when placed in context, can be identified as reflecting child protection practice prior to the publication of three major child abuse inquiries in Britain, namely the Beckford Inquiry (1985), the Carlile Inquiry (1987), and the Cleveland Inquiry (1988). In a study of child care policy up to the 1990s, Parton (1991) traces the evolution of child care from child welfare to child protection, which effectively channelled resources away from general welfare to the identification of 'dangerous' families, a retrograde step in his view. He claimed that social work was now judged through a 'legal or juridical' lens, and that child protection had moved from its medical and social milieu to become a largely forensic activity. This metamorphosis, according to Parton, was largely influenced by the findings of child abuse inquiries.

British child abuse inquiry reports, of which there were over forty-five by the early 1990s, were judged by Reder, Duncan and Gray (1993) to have adopted an accusatory style, grounded in the adversarial framework of the legal system. They considered that the 'blaming' tendency of inquiries was more likely to increase front line workers' defensiveness, rather than help them to examine their roles in difficult cases. Reder *et al.* claim that such investigations said little that is new about how things can go wrong, and did not offer further understanding about how interprofessional communication and co-operation can break down.

They were thus inspired to undertake a retrospective study of inquiry reports, applying a systemic analysis to each case in order to highlight some of the psychological processes which had influenced events, and drawing out common themes. They found that interactional processes within households, within and between professional agencies, and between the families and their professional networks all influenced the evolution of events. The many emotional and relational components of each case could be seen to interact, and influence the course of events. Reder *et al.* identified implications in the work setting, such as the need for more organisational support for staff, provision of adequate resources and guidelines for good practice. They highlighted the frequency of child abuse tragedies occurring when key staff were out sick or on leave, and drew attention to the need to address these occurrences. Furthermore, they emphasised the necessity to pay attention to dynamics between agencies and between professionals, particularly at forums such as case conferences.

The limitations of child abuse inquiries were recognised by the Department of Health (UK) in the late 1980s. After the publication of the Cleveland Inquiry, policy makers in the United Kingdom acknowledged that the inquiries tended to identify the same problems over and over again. At the same time, child abuse statistics were depressingly high and tragedies were still happening. A complete review of the child care system was mooted, and a large investment made in research. Some of the studies which were commissioned are reviewed below, and reflect a new realisation about the direction in which the child protection system has been moving. Also included will be a study by Thorpe (1994) carried out jointly in Britain and Australia.

One of the areas which has received a lot of attention in recent research is the 'consumer' view. This reflects a general move towards partnership with parents, strongly emphasised in the UK *Children Act 1989*. In their inquiry into parental perspectives in child protection, Cleaver and Freeman (1995) set out to examine the degree of concordance between the views of parents and professionals at various stages during the process of investigating allegations of child abuse. Underlying the work is the recognition that societal perceptions of desirable parenting behaviour vary according to expectations within different cultures, leading to a divergence between the attitudes of families and agencies responsible for investigating child abuse.

In an extensive study, the authors monitored the early passage of a large number of abuse allegations through the system over one year. Their findings about the age, gender and family structure of victims and persons believed responsible for the abuse or neglect supported other studies, (see Gibbons, Conroy & Bell, 1995; Thorpe, 1994) reflecting a preponderance of lone parent or reconstituted families, struggling with housing and finance as well as a multitude of personal and child care problems. The children tended to be young, except victims of sexual abuse who came from all age groups. Younger victims were of both sexes but girls predominated in the older age groups. The suspected perpetrators were the children's parents in 70 per cent of all incidents, but this proportion varied according to the type of abuse. Allegations of sexual abuse were attributed to a significant number of non family members as well, though mostly to persons known to the children.

The researchers recognised the difficulty of validating the material collected. The 'truth' about abuse allegations, according to Cleaver and Freeman, contains many 'mobile elements' and what participants consider true may indeed be true for them at that particular moment. They formulated the concept of the *operational perspective*, which is how they termed the 'composite view held at any moment by a participant in an investigation'. Examination of the data highlighted critical events in the development of parents' operational perspectives. These were: (a) the 'confrontation', that is, the first contact between the families and the practitioner investigating the allegation; (b) the case meeting or case conferences at which decisions and plans were made; and (c) certain key moments when new information or changed circumstances could serve to change perceptions.

The findings of Cleaver and Freeman's study suggest that parents experienced very negative reactions to the initial contact with services, feeling trapped, powerless and affronted. Consequently, they often react with defensive and evasive strategies. The researchers conjecture that social workers rely on orthodox and familiar self-presentation in order to cope with the stress of child abuse investigations, and may fail to recognise the anxiety they provoke or the ambiguous messages of control and support that they deliver. They tend to apply a ubiquitous and fault finding framework of assessment, presuming a universal high standard of parenting.

The authors illustrate how case conferences can impact positively or negatively on different aspects of parents' operational perspectives. Evidence suggests that professionals can retreat into conventional guarded role performances, having fashioned an 'inter agency middle class consensus' before the meeting begins, which exacerbates the parents' feelings of embarrassment and disempowerment.

Another significant finding in Cleaver and Freeman's work, which has been replicated in other studies (Farmer & Owen, 1995) is the difference that a change of social worker can make to the family's perception of services and their ability to engage with them. Cleaver and Freeman suggest that this is a way in which parents can correct the imbalance of power in their relationship with professionals.

Cleaver and Freeman suggest that the weight of evidence in their study points to the 'trite sounding conclusion that the closer are the perspectives of all concerned in an investigation of suspected, child abuse, the happier will be the outcome'. Although they found that parents' views could move towards a greater level of concordance with the child protection services, the results indicate that, at the end of the investigation, nearly half the mothers still disputed the professionals' judgement, particularly in sexual abuse cases. This impasse imposes a strong impediment to useful work. The authors suggest that professionals could gain by understanding the benefits of a bargaining process with families by which some middle ground of agreement on culpability could be found, which would foster a relationship. They are also critical of the tendency of social workers to perceive a family situation as better than it is, by their narrow focus on child protection which blinds them to other problems such as marital discord and behavioural problems in the children. In the vast majority of cases, they claim an understanding of the context, meaning and intention is essential to gain the family's confidence in the pursuit of more general welfare objectives.

Cleaver and Freeman claim that the findings in their study highlight the unsuitability of the child protection profession's pre-occupation with categories of abuse, suggesting instead that a differentiated approach to families, according to their circumstances, would be more appropriate. Less stigmatising services could be offered to 'multi problem' and acutely distressed parents who would benefit more from support than surveillance. The authors question what they consider the professional assumption that 'desired outcomes will be secured by following an appropriate administrative route'. They consider that the child protection system has become a 'sophisticated bureaucracy' and that the human disturbance and misplaced resources involved in investigating the majority of allegations is too high a price to pay.

Thorpe (1994), in his study of child protection cases in Australia and Wales, indicated similar concerns about the narrow focus of child protection. His research indicates that the 'work' in social work lies more in moral reasoning, classification and categorisation than in the step-by-step delivery of services suggested by child protection procedures. Thorpe identifies with Dingwall's (1989) theory of 'diagnostic inflation' which suggests that all reported child abuse is equally serious rather than a range of mishaps which includes actual, or potentially, dangerous events.

Thorpe's most significant finding, and one that permeates his analysis of the data, is the degree of moral reasoning employed by child protection workers which ultimately determines what action will ensue. The pattern of intervention reflects not so much concern about the risks faced by children, but judgements about parenting skills, and willingness to co-operate. While problems like addiction are seen as hazardous, case records contain little evidence to suggest that the actual impact of the parental characteristics on the protection and welfare of the children has been considered. Nor is help offered consistently to address specific problems, as the social welfare discourse tends to offer more punitive and short term remedies.

Reflecting on how child abuse work cannot be isolated from cultural and structural issues, Thorpe notes how uncertainties in child protection arise from recent changes in family structure and the ways in which families deal with disagreements. When he considers the situations in which allegations arise, he finds that 20 per cent of child abuse reports are made in the context of marital or family disputes. Thorpe considers that the over-representation of single women parents in the child protection system has more to do with the social construction of their roles than their tendency to abuse or neglect of children. It reinforces his observation that poor and disadvantaged people dispropor-tionately figure in the child protection system, single mothers embodying these categorisations. It also illustrates the extra re-sponsibility women bear for the care of children when parents are not together.

The impact on parents of the investigation process appears as a definitive influence on the subsequent alliances formed by families. Farmer and Owen's study (1995) comprised 44 cases where children were placed on the child protection register. Judgements about parents' caring and protective capacities were often based on the degree of co-operation shown during the early enquiry into child abuse allegations. This is another example of the type of moral reasoning carried out by child protection pro-fessionals, cited by Thorpe (1994), which does not always link the nature of an intervention with the seriousness of the maltreat-ment. Farmer and Owen found that non-abusing mothers were put under severe pressure by the investigation; they were not al-ways told that their children were being interviewed, and their shocked and guilty reactions to the discovery of abuse occluded their ability to protect, in the eyes of professionals. The overriding need to collect evidence for a prosecution was seen by the re-searchers to have a dominating effect on how information was gathered. The authors wondered if the low rate of convictions ob-tained adequately compensated for the potential adverse effects of this forensic activity on the future relationships between child protection workers and families. They suggested that agencies should focus their early interventions on strengthening support systems for the child and should endeavour to minimise the negative effects of their actions. Evidence from the study indicates that, by the end of the investigation, decisions and interventions had crystallised in ways which were likely to determine future outcomes of child care cases.

When the cases were examined longitudinally, the authors found that the longer term management of cases in the study was less clearly executed than the earlier stages. Monitoring arrangements varied considerably; it was assumed that schools would be vigilant and report concerns, though this was rarely established explicitly. The authors found a distinct correlation between the adequacy of the child protection plan and the 'newness' of the case to the social worker. Elements of 'dangerous' professionalism seemed to have permeated the cases which were already open, where social workers had raised their threshold of what was acceptable risk. The tendency of reviews to stick with the original recommendations reinforced this.

Following Cleaver and Freeman (1995) and Thorpe (1994), Farmer and Owen concluded that the intense focus on child protection can lead to a neglect of the wider needs of children and family members; they recognise the contradiction in the increasing use of legalism followed by a low prosecution rate, and its inherent controlling rather than pro-active effect.

In another study, Gibbons, Conroy and Bell describe the operation of the child protection system as a dynamic process, subject to different lay and professional influences at different stages. They identified four phases of the investigation and assessment stage, and the points at which filters would operate to reduce the number of children whose names finally appeared on the child protection register. Evidence from case records suggested that factors associated with the process of selection related to the age and gender of the child, the nature of the abusive incident, previous history, evidence of poverty, illness, and parental 'deviance' such as addiction or criminal record.

The researchers estimated that a quarter of all reported allegations were filtered out with no formal investigation. Despite the fact that situations where neglect was apparent were more likely to reflect families struggling in difficult circumstances, these referrals were more likely than others to be eliminated early. The findings of this study confirm what has been suggested by others, that children and families in the child protection system are subjected to controlling rather than helpful assistance. Consequently, there is little chance of ameliorating their circumstances or attending to their specific needs.

An in-depth study on child protection in one health board area in Ireland was carried out by Buckley (1996) shortly after the implementation of the second part of the *Child Care Act, 1991*, and the publication of the *Report of the Kilkenny Incest Investigation*. The study was exploratory in nature, and sought to qualitatively examine the response of a team of social workers to child abuse and neglect referrals. This research served to highlight the disparity between day-to-day practice and the 'official' discourse of child protection in Ireland, as illustrated in the law, child care policies and child abuse guidelines. It challenged a number of core assumptions inherent in the version of child protection which is claimed to frame practice in the statutory services in Ireland.

The first such assumption is that child protection social workers follow the sort of rational line of action outlined in official procedures when processing child abuse allegations. The study showed that, in practice, several criteria operated to consistently filter referrals out of the system prior to official investigation. One was a 'civil rights' ideal, whereby the social workers were concerned about unnecessarily 'confronting' families as they saw it — intervening in family privacy. This was closely associated with the second main criterion used — the belief that child abuse investigations often did more harm than good, particularly where parents were vulnerable, lacking in confidence and in need of a different type of response. The research showed that instead of automatically entering reports into the system, thereby starting the unstoppable process of investigation, social workers tended to delay action until they could somehow informally or quietly check out the situation without necessarily involving other professionals or even speaking to the family themselves. This process, which in reality breached the child abuse guidelines, satisfied the social workers that they were not taking precipitate action. It also had the advantage of keeping the numbers of investigations at a more manageable level.

The second assumption underlying the official version of child protection in Ireland which was questioned by this study was the willingness of all child care professionals to assume a role in child protection, or to co-ordinate that role with the statutory services. It has already been shown that the issue of inter-agency and inter-professional co-ordination was the focus of much concern in the child abuse inquiry reports. Efforts to improve it were seen to be crucial in ensuring an efficient child protection system, but these endeavours consisted mainly of exhortations or protocols stipulating co-operation rather than making any effort to unpack and address the underlying impediments. The inadequacy of this approach was borne out in the research which indicated, at each stage in the careers of cases, barriers to the communication of child abuse concerns between professionals outside and inside the statutory system: different perceptions of roles and responsibilities, differing professional orientations, lack of trust in the system, fear of over-zealous and insensitive interventions, disagreement about ethical norms such as confidentiality, and sometimes ignorance about way the child protection system worked. Reporting practices were very inconsistent, and there were instances where general practitioners, Gardaí, non-statutory welfare officers and private therapists reported child abuse, but failed to supply the health boards with the contextual information needed to facilitate investigation of the allegations. Many of these referrals were made with ambivalence and almost distaste, reporters not wanting to be identified, or to involve themselves in any depth. In several instances the reporters dropped out of contact before completing the referrals.

The problems with inter-agency and inter-professional co-ordination were closely connected with a third assumption challenged by this study: that case conferences and other inter-agency meetings such as child abuse reviews, which are given such a central position in the machinery of child protection, are effective fora for decision making. In reality, while case conferences were considered useful and beneficial at times, there is strong evidence to show that the powerful interactional processes at these meetings tended to deflect energy and attention away from the interests of families and children, and that interventions were frequently planned around inter-agency conflicts rather than focused on the presenting risks or concerns of the families involved.

The key point in this study, then, is the contrast between the *reality* of child protection practice which is exposed when these activities are seen in context, and the *desire* for 'certainty' which is creeping into the public and managerial perception and *expectations* of what is achievable to address child abuse in Ireland.

What recent studies have demonstrated is that while child care services have undoubtedly become more organised, better resourced, and essentially, more effective in protecting children from harm and neglect, this is not without considerable cost. There are concerns about the bureaucratised and narrow focus of the work which is frequently practised from a defensive perspective that seeks to protect workers and agencies as much as it does children. There is also anxiety that the child protection discourse is developing without sufficient reference to those whose duty it is to operationalise it, and those whose needs it seeks to meet. It is all the more timely to conduct and exploration of the area, to make visible the true nature of the work, and by so doing, to highlight aspects of practice that may be usefully addressed.

OBJECTIVES OF THE BOOK

Drawing on the research described above which reported a high number of poor and marginalised families in referrals to social workers, who only received a service if their problems could be defined in terms of child abuse, it was decided to explore the nature of referrals to the social work service in the South Eastern Health Board, to see if reports of child abuse and neglect elicited a different type of response to other referrals. Following the evaluations of the child protection system offered by Farmer and Owen (1995) and Gibbons, Conroy and Bell (1995), we considered it important to focus on the practitioners' perceptions of the efficacy of the various aspects of 'child protection machinery' which have recently been implemented in the South Eastern Health Board region. In particular, given the emphasis placed on inter-agency and inter-professional co-ordination in the Irish system, both in research and in the recent inquiry reports, we decided to examine co-operation as an issue, and also to reflect on the child protection network as consisting of a wide range of professionals. Most importantly, we considered it vital to include the perspectives of parents and carers, in an attempt to highlight the current state of 'partnership'. In summary, the research aimed to explore:

- The nature of referrals to the social work service of the South Eastern Health Board

- The nature of child abuse and neglect notifications made to the South Eastern Health Board

- The initial response of the service to clients

- The use and efficacy of child abuse guidelines and procedures, and the official stages of child protection activity within the Board (Child Abuse Notification Meetings, Case conferences, child protection plans)

- The role of social workers in child protection

- The roles and responsibilities of the full range of professionals in the child protection network

- Inter-agency and inter-professional co-ordination

- Parental perspectives in child protection cases

- A general view of the current state of child protection systems.

These themes are all inter-related and feature consistently throughout the study.

THE LOCATION

The South Eastern Health Board covers the counties of Carlow, Kilkenny, Tipperary South Riding, Wexford and Waterford. At the 1991 Census, the population of the region was 383,188. According to the Census, 33.7 per cent of the population were aged 17 and under. Notifications of child abuse have paralleled national trends with a substantial increase over the past number of years as seen by Figure 1.3.

FIGURE 1.3: CHILD ABUSE NOTIFICATIONS TO THE SOUTH EASTERN
HEALTH BOARD, 1992–1995

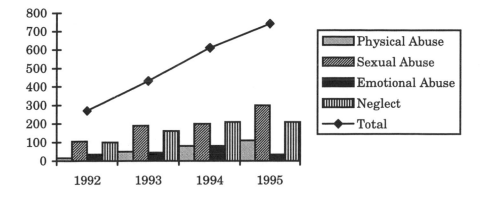

Since the *Child Care Act, 1991* and the publication of the Kilkenny Incest Investigation, the number of social staff employed by
the Board has increased; community child care workers were
employed for the first time ever in 1994; a specialist fostering
service was developed and greater co-ordination between Gardaí
and the Health Board fostered.

METHODOLOGY

The methodology utilised in this study is one which aimed to gen-
erate a perspective on the operation of the child protection system
in the South Eastern Health Board, rather than a methodology
which sought to test competing theories of child protection effectiveness, using standardised measuring instruments. Thus, the
broad objective of the research was to analyse the case load of social work teams in the South Eastern Health Board, and to examine in detail the perspectives of the actors (parents, guardians,
social workers, child care workers, psychologists, public health
nurses, teachers, Gardaí, etc.) involved in a small number of child
abuse cases. By utilising such an interpretative perspective, the
research aimed to explore the diversity of meanings and significance of events which the different actors in the system attach for
objectively similar situations. The analysis of events and recommendations put forward are generated through interpreting these

interactions between different stakeholders in the child protection system. The quantitative data gathered attempted to outline the contours of the child protection system; to map out the location of child abuse cases in the overall context of the workload of social workers and place the qualitative material in context.

The collection of the data from the case records of all referrals to social work teams in the South Eastern Health Board formed the initial phase of the research or *Phase One* as we refer to it throughout this book.

The second phase of the research referred to as *Phase Two* in the book explored many of the issues that emerged from Phase One and provides the necessary detail that illustrates the complexity of child protection procedures.

The months of May and June 1995 were selected as the study period. As the social work service tends to be the 'gateway' and primary filter of child abuse and neglect cases, allegations which were notified[5] to this service during this two-month period were documented. In order to place these reports in context, a census of all referrals to the social work service during this period was carried out. We refer to the general referrals to the social work service of the South Eastern Health Board in the said period as *GRSWSs*. The child abuse and neglect notifications made during this period are referred to as *CANNs*.

In total, there were 423 referrals to the social work service during the period selected for study. Information was collected concerning the socio-economic status of the families, the reason for referral, path of referral, circumstances in the family at the time of referral, immediate action taken, services offered, and ultimate disposal of cases. Data concerning 118 CANNs were collected by the researchers, using specially designed data sheets, to which information from case files and intake sheets was transferred. Information was again collected on the socio-economic circumstances of families, reason for referral, and path of referral.

---

[5] Under the Department of Health Child Abuse Guidelines 1987, (p. 9) 'Any person who knows or suspects that a child is being harmed, or is at risk of harm, has a duty to convey his concern to the local Health Board'. Notifications' in the South Eastern Health Board are made to the Director of Community Care by the completion of a specific notification form.

Problems already present in the family, and services already involved with the family were ascertained. Immediate responses were noted, including the use of child abuse procedures. Data were also collected on the use of case conferences and the construction of child protection plans. This part of the research (i.e. analysis of GRSWS (423) and CANNs (118), which we have called Phase One) was completed between October and November 1995.

Some of the information we sought was not routinely recorded and therefore was not available on either the intake sheets or in the case files.

In Phase Two of the study, a qualitative methodology was utilised to explore in greater detail the process of child protection from a number of different perspectives. The second phase of the study was carried out between February and March 1996, and sought to collect more detailed information on the child protection investigative process and on the longer term management of child abuse cases. Social workers, parents and at least one other professional involved in each case were interviewed. Eighteen child abuse and neglect cases were selected from the 118 CANNs made to the Health Board in May/June 1995. These cases were selected by the researchers in consultation with the social work managers in the region. The rationale for their selection was that:

- They were still 'open'

- They had a number of professionals involved, and

- That they were spread evenly throughout the region and allocated to different social workers.

Personal interviews, using semi-structured questionnaires, were carried out with the social worker and at least one other professional involved in each case. We also interviewed the parent or parents in fourteen out of the eighteen cases. The interview schedule covered similar areas to that of the social workers. The principal focus was on inter-agency co-operation, practitioners' perceptions of their child protection roles, their knowledge of child abuse procedures, and their views on the child protection system in general. In all, fifty-two personal interviews were carried out in Phase Two of the study.

By utilising two complementary research methodologies, a detailed picture of the operation of the child protection system in the South Eastern Health Board is discernible. The diverse range of issues that social workers encounter in a two month period contextualises the role of child protection within the overall responsibilities of social workers in the South Eastern Health Board. By focusing on a select number of child abuse cases, the methodology has allowed us to understand the complexity, diversity and interaction of professionals and parents in child protection work.

CONCLUSION

The *Child Care Act, 1991,* along with the proposed amendment to the Act which will give health boards the power to detain children, forms the conceptual and legislative framework in which child care experts deploy their skills in promoting the welfare of children. The legislation has been supplemented by a series of guidelines on the management of child protection and the responsibilities of the various agencies involved. Yet despite its long gestation in becoming an operational reality, the implications of the Act for child care experts and their clients have yet to be fully explored. The interaction of child care legislation and the role of child care experts with other societal trends also needs greater elaboration. There is an underlying assumption in much that has been written about the Act that its enactment is a positive development, yet a small number of studies of the Act in operation have suggested that substantial gaps exist between the aspirations of the Act and its operational reality (O'Doherty, 1996; O'Sullivan, 1995a, 1996). More fundamentally, the ideological and historical evolution of child welfare services in Ireland, in addition to the discourses that have shaped our current child welfare arrangements are as yet substantially undeveloped (although see Ferguson, 1993, 1996; and Gilligan, 1989, 1996, for some attempts to interpret the current rapid changes in child welfare). As a consequence, there is a lack of understanding of why our child welfare services are developing in precisely the manner in which they are. The accelerated rate of change in the nature of child welfare services in Ireland and their precise form owe as much to historical contingencies as they reflect modern concerns regarding the promotion of the welfare of the child. We need to be mindful that we should not adopt a linear model of child welfare services in Ireland, whereby we see each development as a welcome break from the past and increasing our concern for children. The increased power that the *Child Care Act, 1991* gives to child welfare experts may be abused and more covert forms of institutional discrimination and abuse may emerge. Although this current work is not an evaluation of the operation of the *Child Care Act*, it does, nevertheless, offer some perspectives on the operation of aspects of the child care system in one health board area.

Chapter Two offers a profile of the referrals made to the social work service during the study period, along with a profile of the child abuse and neglect notifications made to the Board during the same period. It describes the initial response made, along with more detailed data which was collected on the child abuse and neglect referrals. Chapter Three examines the specific involvement of social workers in the child protection process from initial investigation to on-going case management. Chapter Four considers the roles and responsibilities of various other key professionals in the child protection system. Chapter Five examines the nature of inter-agency and inter-professional relations in the Board. Chapter Six looks at the operation, role and functions of case conferences in the board. Chapter Seven examines the level of partnership between social workers and families, and offers the perspectives of parents. Chapter Eight considers the child protection system more generally, focusing on procedures and policy. Finally Chapter Nine summarises and concludes the findings throughout the study. It is important to emphasise from the outset that, while the study is outlined in discrete chapters, much of the findings are inter-linked and need to be viewed in that context.

CHAPTER TWO

PHASE ONE FINDINGS:
PROFILE OF GENERAL REFERRALS AND CHILD ABUSE
NOTIFICATIONS TO THE SOUTH EASTERN HEALTH BOARD
SOCIAL WORK SERVICE IN MAY AND JUNE 1995

INTRODUCTION

As outlined earlier, this study was carried out in two parts, referred to as Phase One and Phase Two. In Phase One, data was collected in relation to (a) general referrals to the social work service (GRSWSs) of the South Eastern Health Board during the study period (May and June, 1995),[1] and (b) child abuse and neglect notifications[2] (CANNs) made during the same period.[3] A certain proportion of the CANNs were new referrals and are therefore also represented in the 423 GRSWSs. However, some of the CANNs relate to cases which were already open but where a new child abuse or neglect concern was discovered and notified.

The aim of Phase One was to provide contextual information on which to base the more detailed analysis of cases in Phase Two. More specifically, this phase provided information on the socio-economic status of clients referred to the South Eastern Health Board and the path and nature in both the GRSWS and CANN category. Phase One also aimed to provide some prelimi-

---

[1] This data was collected by the social workers themselves from their intake books. An 'Intake sheet' is a single, official form upon which a brief record of the referral is made by social workers

[2] A 'notification' is made when a report of child abuse or neglect is officially brought to the attention of the Senior Social Worker, the Director of Community Care, and the Superintendent Public Health Nurse.

[3] As outlined in Chapter One, CANN refers to all notifications of child abuse and neglect which were made in the period May/June 1995. This data was collected by the researchers from social workers case files. 'Case Files' are the combined records kept by social workers on each case

nary findings in relation to the initial stages of child abuse and neglect investigations which sets the context for the more in-depth qualitative research findings presented in Phase Two. The following are the main findings deriving from Phase One of our research.[4]

Section One provides a summary of the socio-economic charac-teristics of both GRSWSs and CANNs to the Health Board. Sec-tion Two outlines our findings in relation to the nature and path of referrals and notifications, and Section Three outlines in more detail the path of CANNs over the initial investigative stage.[5] This stage includes the initial response of the Health Board to notifications of child abuse and neglect, preliminary plans of in-tervention and early interventions with children and families. As outlined above, Phase Two considers this stage of intervention in more depth in relation to a selection of CANNs from Phase One, as well as going onto consider the on-going process of interven-tion.

As explained in Chapter Two, social work records were not de-signed for research purposes, and in certain instances, not all the information requested on the data sheets in relation to both GRSWSs and CANNs were provided. As a consequence, some data were more readily available than others. Detailed tables contain-ing the data collected are provided throughout the chapter.

SECTION ONE: SOCIO-ECONOMIC CHARACTERISTICS OF PERSONS REFERRED TO THE SERVICE IN GENERAL, AND CHILD ABUSE AND NEGLECT IN PARTICULAR

In order to build up a profile of referrals to the social work service of the South Eastern Health Board, information was collected

---

[4] As the 118 CANN are not a direct sample from the 423 GRSWS as some of the notification were made on cases which were already open, it is not pos-sible to make direct comparisons between the findings from each category. However, it is possible to present some findings collectively, as they shared certain commonalties. This will be done, where appropriate, throughout the chapter.

[5] As discussed in Chapter One, a more detailed analysis of CANN referrals was made in Phase One in order to provide a contextual basis for the quali-tative analysis in Phase Two of 18 cases from the 118 CANN sample.

concerning the socio-economic characteristics of clients. To ascertain the socio-economic status of persons referred, we explored four main areas which we considered to be key indicators: family composition, employment status of parents or carers in the families, housing status, and possession or otherwise of a medical card. More specifically, we sought to compare socio-economic circumstances of clients referred to the South Eastern Health Board social work service with those of the general population.

A key finding from this part of the research was that the socio-economic circumstances of individuals and families in the GRSWS category were remarkably similar to those represented in the CANN category. However, a remarkable divergence was found between the socio-economic characteristics of clients involved with the SEHB and those in the general population of the South Eastern Health Board region. The following is a summary of the key findings in relation to socio-economic circumstances of clients represented in both the GRSWS category and in the CANN categories.

Firstly, in relation to the *family composition* of both the 423 GRSWSs and the 118 CANNs, the most frequently represented unit was that of the two parent/carer family. The second most prevalent unit was lone parent headed families, which accounted for over a quarter of clients. The vast majority of lone parents were female. The key difference between the general referrals and child abuse notifications is that, of the former, a number of single adults and adult couples without children were also referred, whereas all child abuse notifications comprised of at least one parent and one child[6] (see Tables 2.1 & 2.2). The most significant finding in relation to family composition was the high proportion of lone parents involved with the SEHB in comparison to their representation in the general community. In 1991, the percentage of lone parents in the population in general was 10.7 per cent (Census of Population, 1991) whereas 28 per cent of GRSWSs and 30 per cent of CANNs were made up of lone parent families. Current research has shown that lone parents are likely to have incomes that are low by the standards of Irish society at large

---

[6] As one would expect, given the fact that CANN referrals relate specifically to families where children are, or may be, at risk.

(McCashin, 1996) thus suggesting that the disproportionately high percentage of lone parents represents one indicator of low economic status.

TABLE 2.1: FAMILY STRUCTURE OF REFERRALS TO THE SEHB IN GRSWSS

Family Structure	% Cases Referred to the SEHB (n=423)
Two adult carers	48
Female lone parent	25
Male lone parent	3
Other relatives	0
Foster parent(s)	1
Adult couple with no children	3
Single adult male	2
Single adult female	11
Other	6
Total	100

TABLE 2.2: FAMILY COMPOSITION (CANNS)

Family Structure	% Notifications of Child Abuse / Neglect (n=118)
Two adult carers	65
Lone parent	30
Other relatives	2
Foster parent(s)	1
Other	2
Total	100

The second socio-economic determinant examined was the *employment status* of persons referred to the service. The employment status of males and females was considered separately. The available data shows that at least 20 per cent of adult males in the GRSWS category were unemployed. Given the fact that one third of households in this category had no adult male, this meant that unemployment featured in at least a third of all households where an adult male was present. Likewise, in the CANN category, a high proportion of male carers were unemployed. Taking account of the fact that one-fifth of families were headed by lone female parents, it was found that almost one-third of fathers in families in this category were unemployed (see Tables 2.3 & 2.4). Comparison of employment figures of the South Eastern population in general with those receiving social work service from the Health Board illuminates the relatively low level of employment among persons referred to the social work service; the 1995 *Labour Force Survey* shows that 85 per cent of the overall population in the South East were employed full-time (Central Statistics Office, 1995), whereas only 15 per cent of households in the GRSWS category and 25 per cent of households represented in the CANN category had a male member in full-time employment.

The area of employment of female carers likewise reflects a low level of employment among women referred to the SEHB. However, findings relating to employment status of women must be treated with care. From the data available, it was found that of female carers within the GRSWS category, 14 per cent of female carers were unemployed and 43 per cent were full-time parents, while CANN findings suggest that 1 per cent of women were unemployed and 59 per cent were full-time in the home. It must be borne in mind that where mothers or female carers were concerned, the distinction between 'full time parent' and 'unemployed' was made in the context of little other information being available, and on the subjective judgement of the social workers completing the data sheets. It seems more appropriate therefore to note that less than one-fifth of female carers from both samples were employed outside of the home in any capacity. Female carers were found to be employed full-time in only approximately one-tenth of both GRSWSs and CANNs. A further small percentage of women were recorded as working part-time or as self-employed in both samples.

TABLE 2.3: EMPLOYMENT STATUS OF PERSONS REFERRED IN
GRSWSS (N = 423)

Employment Status	% Females Referred to SEHB Service	% Males Referred to SEHB Service
Full time	6	15
Occasional	2	3
Part-time	8	2
Long-term disability	0	3
Self-employed	1	1
Unemployed	14	20
Full-time parent	43	0
Not applicable	7	33
Other	2	3
Missing	18	20
Total	100[7]	100

TABLE 2.4: EMPLOYMENT STATUS OF FAMILY MEMBERS (CANNS)
(N = 118)

Employment Status	% Female Carers	% Male Carers
Full time	8	25
Occasionally	3	1
Part-time	6	1
Long term disability	0	4
Self-employed	0	3
Unemployed	1	25
Full-time parent	59	4
Not applicable	7	17
Other	0	3
Missing	16	17
Total	100	100

The *possession of a medical card* was considered to be another
useful indicator of socio-economic circumstances, given the fact

---

[7] As outlined in the methodology, not all of the tables add up to exactly 100
per cent, but figures are rounded up to the nearest whole number.

that a person must be within a certain means to be eligible. The intake sheets used by social workers have a section on whether or not clients are in possession of medical cards. However, this information was not recorded in approximately one-fifth of GRSWS and one third of CANN data sheets. From the data available, at least two-thirds of persons referred were in possession of a medical card in comparison to just over one-third (37.9 per cent) of the general population (see Tables 2.5 and 2.6).

TABLE 2.5: NUMBER OF CLIENTS WITH MEDICAL CARDS (GRSWSS) (N = 423)

Possession of a Medical Card	% Persons Referred to SEHB Social Work Service
Yes	64
No	14
Not applicable	1
Missing	21
Total	100

TABLE 2.6: NUMBER OF FAMILIES IN POSSESSION OF MEDICAL CARDS (CANNS) (N = 118)

Possession of a Medical Card	% Persons Referred
Yes	46
No	17
Not applicable	2
Information Missing	36
Total	100

Housing status was the final indicator of families' social and economic circumstances which we analysed. We found that two-fifths of clients in the GRSWS category and half of the CANN sample lived in local authority accommodation. One tenth of GRSWSs and 6 per cent of CANNs were found to live in rented accommodation while less than a quarter of persons in both samples owned their own house. A small minority, under one tenth, lived in alternative accommodation such as mobile homes or caravans (see

Tables 2.7 & 2.8). These findings suggest that the housing status of persons referred to the social work service of the SEHB differs significantly to the housing circumstances of the population in general where, in 1991, 81 per cent of the population of the South East owned their own homes and 10 per cent of the population lived in local authority housing (Census of Population, 1991).

TABLE 2.7: HOUSING SITUATION OF THOSE REFERRED IN GRSWSS (N = 423)

Status of Family Home	% Persons Referred to SEHB Social Work Service
Family Owned	18
Rented from local authority	37
Rented from private landlord	11
Not applicable	3
Other	8
Not available	22
Total	100

TABLE 2.8: HOUSING CIRCUMSTANCES OF FAMILIES IN THE CANNS CATEGORY (N = 118)

Status of Family Home	% Persons Referred
Family owned	23
Rented from local authority	47
Rented from private landlord	6
Not applicable	1
Other	8
Not available	15
Total	100

While, it is important to note that socio-economic status can be used to refer to such a broad range of arenas that it is difficult to set down criteria for its measurement, we consider the four above categories to represent significant indicators as to the socio-economic circumstances of a population. Despite the lack of information available in a number of instances, the findings available strongly suggest that on the whole, the persons referred to the social work service of the SEHB for both general issues and child abuse and neglect come from significantly more socio-economically deprived circumstances relative to the South Eastern population in general. Other similar research studies in both Ireland (McKeown & Gilligan, 1991) and England (Farmer & Owen, 1995; Gibbons, Conroy & Bell, 1995) likewise suggest that persons referred to the Health Board/Social Services generally derive from a relatively poor socio-economic background. This finding however does not suggest that persons from socially deprived backgrounds are most likely to abuse or neglect their children. Rather, as has been previously recognised in research (Dingwall, Eekelaar & Murray; 1983), persons of limited financial and material means depend more on public services to meet their health and housing needs. This leaves them more open to scrutiny, so that abuse and neglect of their children can be identified more easily. The findings do however suggest a strong correlation between low socio-economic status and referral to the health board for child abuse and neglect, or more general family problems.

SECTION TWO: PATH AND NATURE OF REFERRALS AND NOTIFICATIONS TO THE SEHB

By 'referral path' we mean the way in which GRSWSs and CANNs[8] reach the social work services initially. The most common process was found to be referral of individuals or families by other professionals, family members, concerned relatives or neighbours/members of the local community. Social Workers themselves were rarely identified as the main referrer of either GRSWSs or CANNs. Rather, social workers' primary point of contact with the cases was their response to and follow up of the various referrals. A number of key findings emanate from our analysis of the path

---

[8] The distinction between notifications and referrals is important to keep in mind here. 'Referrals' of child abuse and neglect were reports made to staff in the Board by various people, about their suspicions of abuse in different situations. 'Notification' of child abuse and neglect was the process by which these reports were *officially* made to managers in the Board, following the child abuse procedures, and by use of official 'child abuse notification forms'.

of referrals to the social work service of the SEHB. In some instances, the path of both general referrals and child abuse notifications reflected similar findings with some notable divergences.

In relation to general referrals (GRSWSs) the study revealed
that professionals working with individuals and families were the
most frequent referrers to the service. They accounted for forty-
two per cent of all GRSWSs. Of those professionals, those who
most frequently referred persons and families to the social work
service were various practitioners from what we term community
based 'generic' services such as schools, GPs, public health nurses
and Gardaí (Table 2.9). Professional referrals of child abuse and
neglect (CANN) were even higher at 60 per cent. Similar to
GRSWSs, of cases referred in the CANN category, it was primarily
practitioners within the community, who were offering a generic
service to families, who made such referrals (see Table 2.10).

TABLE 2.9: SOURCE OF REFERRAL (GRSWSs) (N = 423)

Referrer	% Referrals to SEHB Social Work Service
School	9
GP	5
Gardaí	4
Public health nurse	7
Child psychiatrist	1
Hospital	13
Medical social worker	1
Area Medical Officer	1
Psychologist	1
Community Care social worker	5
Both parents	12
Self	18
Neighbour	3
Other member of public	1
Anonymous	5

TABLE 2.10: SOURCE OF REFERRALS OF CHILD ABUSE AND NEGLECT
TO THE SEHB (CANNS)

Source of Referral	%
School	20
GP	10
Gardaí	5
Public Health Nurse	4
Child Psychiatrist	3
Residential Care Worker	2
Community Care Worker	2
Hospital	-
Medical Social Worker	-
Ophthalmologist	1
Paediatrician	2
Refuge Worker	2
Area Medical Officer	-
CSA Unit	1
Play Group Leader	1
Psychologist	0
Community Care Social Worker	6
Mother Only	9
Father Only	2
Both Parents	2
Other Relative	9
Self	1
Neighbour	5
Other Member of Public	2
Anonymous	13
Other	18
Missing	1

Where referrals of both GRSWSs and CANNs were made by professionals, it was most likely to be the result of the professional
themselves identifying an individual or family difficulty, such as
alleged child abuse or neglect or behavioural problems in children, during direct contact with individuals or families. The other
key trigger for professional referrals was where a child or parent

had disclosed it to them. In most instances therefore, it was services already involved with certain families at the time of contact
who were responsible for the majority of referrals made by professionals in both samples. The high rate of referrals by generic
professionals, such as teachers, public health nurses, GPs and
Gardaí support this point.[9] This crucial role of generic professional referrals is particularly relevant in relation to child abuse
and neglect referrals which were most frequently identified by
practitioners, whose professional tasks bring them into contact
with children and families on a frequent basis, or by members of
the public, who encounter suspicions in their neighbourhood or
within their families. Community Care social workers are therefore primarily dependent on the ability and willingness of other
professionals to identify abuse and communicate their concerns to
the statutory services.

   This point is illuminated in the finding that Community Care
social workers themselves are recorded as having made only 5 per
cent of the general referrals (GRSWS category) and 6 per cent of
the child abuse and neglect referrals which were notified (CANN
category), most of which constituted a transfer of referrals from
other areas rather than the social workers themselves initiating
the contact. The identification and referral of abuse and neglect,
as well as more general individual and family difficulties by professionals, are therefore crucial aspects of the social work service
in general, and the child protection system in particular.[10]

   In addition to referrals from professionals, a number of referrals of both categories came from parents themselves, which made
just over 10 per cent of referrals in both samples.[11] The most significant difference in the path of general referrals and child abuse
referrals which were notified were found to be: (a) the higher pro-

---

[9] For example, school referrals in particular frequently followed disclosures
from children to their class teachers or principle while many of the reports
from general practitioners followed discussions from concerned parents.

[10] The nature of professional involvement, other than social work, is considered in detail in Phase Two of the research.

[11] This relates to parents making referrals on behalf of their children in relation to a problem experienced by the child themselves.

portion of self-referrals[12] made in GRSWSs (18 per cent) in comparison to 1 per cent of CANNs; and (b) the higher likelihood of referrals being made by concerned relatives, members of the public and anonymous callers in relation to child abuse and neglect referrals in comparison to general referrals to the service (see Tables 2.9 & 2.10). These findings suggest that individuals and families are more likely to make contact themselves with the services in relation to problems *other* than alleged child abuse and neglect. They highlight again the dependence of the social work service on the identification and reporting of alleged child abuse and neglect by persons within the community. They also demonstrate the reactive nature of the social work service at present and confirm that it is other professionals, family members and lay persons within the community who are making the initial definitions of what constitutes a difficulty (family or individual), and who make decisions as to what constitutes a case of child abuse and neglect which requires some form of official response. It is only when the cases have actually been defined as a problem and thus referred to the service that social workers begin to screen them and make decisions as to what response the referrals should receive.

The question which derives directly from the above findings, is: what are the nature of referrals made to the social work service of the SEHB by the various referrers? In order to excavate the nature of such referrals in more depth, we explored the following key areas in relation to both samples:

- the range of reasons for referral;

- whether other problems were being experienced by the individual/family at the time of referral;

- the type of services which were offered, initially, in response to the referrals.

As one would expect, general referrals constituted a broader *range of reasons for referral* to that of referrals represented in the CANN category. Tables 2.11 & 2.12 summarise the range of rea-

---

[12] These would be referrals where an adult is the potential client or where an older child makes a referral regarding a personal or family problem.

sons for referral in relation to both categories. GRSWSs were made for a variety of reasons. These included child abuse and neglect, behavioural problems in children, effects of drug and alcohol abuse, parents' inability to cope, parental disharmony, lack of family supports, homelessness, parental illness, financial problems, and a range of other family crises. The largest single group concerned child abuse[13] and neglect, which represented one-third of the identified reasons for referral (see Table 2.11).

TABLE 2.11: REASON FOR REFERRAL TO THE SOCIAL WORK SERVICE OF THE SEHB IN GRSWSS

Reason for Referral	% Referrals to Social Work Service
Behavioural problems in children	10
Physical abuse	8
Sexual abuse	13
Emotional abuse	3
Neglect	11
Parents unable to cope	9
Parental disharmony	15
Child out of control	4
Child abandoned	1
Parental illness – physical	2
Parental illness – mental	4
Alcohol abuse	2
Substance abuse	9
Other family crisis	7
Immature parenting	6
Lack of family and other supports	5
Pregnancy counselling	7
Tracing	1
Fostering information	1
Adoption information	1
Homeless	5
Adolescent problems	3
Financial problems	7
Other	28

---

[13] This includes the category of sexual, physical and emotional abuse.

All referrals which resulted in notification (i.e. those in the CANN category) related to some form of alleged child abuse or neglect. Almost half of all child abuse and neglect notifications concerned sexual abuse. One-third of all notifications were related to child neglect and a further quarter were referred for physical abuse. Emotional abuse was the lowest category of abuse notified. It accounted for 14 per cent of all cases (see Table 2.12).

TABLE 2.12: REASONS FOR REFERRALS OF CHILD ABUSE AND NEGLECT (CANNS)

Reason for Referral	%
Behavioural problems in children	2
Physical abuse	26
Sexual abuse	47
Emotional abuse	14
Neglect	31
Parents unable to cope	1
Parental disharmony	0
Child out of control	0
Child abandoned	3
Parental illness – physical	0
Parental illness – mental	1
Addictions	2
Other family crisis	0
Immature parenting	2
Lack of family and other supports	1
Pregnancy counselling	1
Adolescent problems	1
Other	3

In over half of the general referrals to the social work service, just one of the above problems was offered as the primary reason for contact. In a quarter of the 423 cases, there were two main reasons for referral and in almost one-fifth of the families, three or more reasons for referral were cited (see Table 2.13).

TABLE 2.13: NUMBER OF REASONS FOR REFERRAL IN GRSWSS

Number of Reasons for Referral to SEHB Social Work Service	% Persons Referred to SEHB Social Work Service (n = 423)
One	59
Two	24
Three	10
Four	3
More than four	2
Zero	2
Total	100

As in the case of GRSWSs, in a number of instances, there was more than one reason for referral of cases within the CANN category. In over one-fifth of notifications, two forms of abuse were mentioned. In a further fifth, in addition to child abuse and neglect, at least one other reason for referral to the service was identified. These included, for example, parenting difficulties, lack of social supports, and children's behavioural problems. Only in a minority of cases were three or more reasons for referral given in the CANN category (see Tables 2.14.1, 2.14.2).

TABLE 2.14.1: INCIDENCE OF MORE THAN ONE FORM OF ABUSE OR NEGLECT REFERRED TO SEHB SOCIAL WORK SERVICE

Type of Abuse	Percentage Referrals
Child sexual abuse/Emotional abuse	3
Emotional abuse/Neglect	5
Child sexual abuse/Neglect	3
Physical abuse/Neglect	5
Physical abuse/Emotional abuse	5
Physical abuse/Child sexual abuse	1
TOTAL	22%

TABLE 2.14.2: NUMBER OF REASONS FOR REFERRAL OTHER THAN
CHILD ABUSE AND NEGLECT

Number of Other Reasons for Referral to SEHB Social Work Service	*Percentage Referrals (n = 118)*
No other reason	74
One	21
Two	2
Three-Four	3
Total	100

In order to explore further the nature of referrals to the social welfare service of the SEHB, the presence of other problems at the time of referral was explored. In both categories, it was most likely that at least one other individual or family difficulty was identified as being present at the time of the referral. From the information available on the data sheets in relation to GRSWS, it appears that in almost 80 per cent of cases at least one other problem existed, and in approximately one-quarter, up to two or three other problems were found to exist. A small proportion of families presented with multiple problems at the time of referral (see Table 2.15). Referrals represented in the CANN category likewise demonstrate the existence of other identified difficulties for families referred. Three-quarters of case records in the CANN category mentioned at least one other problem in the family at the time of referral. It was more likely in this category for families to be experiencing multiple problems. Of the child abuse notifications, in approximately 10 per cent of cases, it was found that six or more other problems were present in the family at the time of referral (see Table 2.16).[14]

---

[14] Although the different method of data collection for GRSWSs and CANNs must be taken into account here. GRSWS data was collected from the more limited information source of referral forms, whereas CANN data derived from a fuller analysis of case files.

TABLE 2.15: NUMBER OF OTHER PROBLEMS PRESENT AT TIME OF
REFERRAL IN GRSWSS

Number of Problems Present	*% Referrals to Social Work Service (n = 423)*
None	21
One	41
Two	16
Three	11˙
Four	6
Five	3
Six – Ten	2

TABLE 2.16: NUMBER OF OTHER PROBLEMS PRESENT AT TIME OF
REFERRAL OF CHILD ABUSE AND NEGLECT

Number of Problems Present	*Sample 2 (n = 118)*
None	24
One	22
Two	18
Three	13
Four	8
Five	4
Six – Ten	11

In both categories, the range of such problems was extremely
broad. Child abuse and neglect was identified as 'another problem' present in almost a quarter of GRSWSs. Other significant
problems were identified as parental disharmony, parenting difficulties, alcohol or drug abuse and lack of family or other supports
(see Table 2.17). Similarly, the range of other problems present at
the time of referral for cases represented in the CANN category
included marital problems, behavioural difficulties in children,
parenting difficulties, alcohol abuse, and physical or mental dis-
ability (see Table 2.18). This finding suggests that the majority of
persons referred to the SEHB social work service were experiencing significant, and in many cases multiple, family difficulties relating to both the nature of the referral and other problems pres-

ent at that time. It was more likely for families represented in the CANN category to be experiencing a number of other problems than those in the GRSWS category, but the nature of the problems present were similar for both groups and covered a broad range of individual and family difficulties.

TABLE 2.17: RANGE OF PROBLEMS PRESENT AT TIME OF REFERRAL IN GRSWS

Problem Type	*% of Referrals to Social Work Service*
Behaviour problems	12
Physical abuse	5
Sexual abuse	7
Emotional abuse	4
Neglect	8
Parenting difficulties	13
Parental disharmony	21
Parental illness (physical)	3
Parental illness (mental)	4
Immature parenting	10
Child out of control	5
Adolescent problems	5
Alcohol abuse	11
Other substance abuse	1
Other family crisis	6
Lack of family or other supports	9
Homeless	5
Pregnancy counselling	6
Tracing	1
Fostering information	1
Adoption information	1
Financial problems	9
Other	13

TABLE 2.18: RANGE OF OTHER PROBLEMS PRESENT AT TIME OF
REFERRAL

Problem Type	Percentage Referrals (n = 118)
Behaviour problems	25
Physical abuse	10
Sexual abuse	14
Emotional abuse	4
Neglect	21
Parenting difficulties	22
Family violence	9
Marital problems	22
Parental illness (physical)	2
Parental illness (mental)	1
Alcohol abuse	13
Other substance abuse	4
Lack of family or other supports	8
Homeless	3
Inadequate housing	12
Financial problems	9
Inconsistent school attendance	2
Physical/Mental disability	12
Criminal record	1
Other	14

Another indicator of problems present at the time of referral was
considered to be the involvement of other 'helping' services with
the individual or family at the time of referral.[15] Of the GRSWS
category, schools were involved with almost a quarter of the families in relation to personal issues other than day-to-day teaching;
for instance, special learning needs, concerns about neglect, behaviour problems, and poor attendance. Both the Gardaí and
hospital services were also found to have specific involvement
with approximately one-fifth of persons referred. In one-tenth of

---

[15] By this we are referring to services dealing with a specific problem as opposed to a general day-to-day involvement of services such as schools, public
health nurses (in the case of families with young children) or GPs.

cases, a child of the family was attending a Special School. Various specialist services, such as the Community Child Centre, Psychology, Community Child Care Workers, Adult Psychiatry and Family Support Work Service were involved in a minority of families at the time of referral (see Table 2.19).

TABLE 2.19: OTHER SERVICES INVOLVED WITH FAMILY AT TIME OF REFERRAL IN GRSWS

Other Services	*No. of Cases*
Gardaí	17
School	23
Hospital	18
Child Psychiatry Services	2
Special School	10
CSA Unit	2
Psychology	5
Community Child Care Worker	2
Family Support Worker	2
Adult Psychiatry	8
Day Care	2
Other	26

In relation to child abuse and neglect referrals which were subsequently notified (CANN category), as well as considering other services involved with the family at the time of referral, we looked for evidence of previous contact between the families concerned and the South Eastern Health Board social work service.[16] It was found that almost half of families represented in the CANN category had had previous contact with the social work service. Many of those cases were already open and the majority of the remainder had contact with the social work service within the past year. Ten per cent of families had contact over one year ago. A number of the 'previously known' families also had contact with other child care services at the time of referral. These were most com-

---

[16] In order to ascertain if previous child abuse or neglect concerns had existed in the family.

monly community-based generic services such as schools, which were involved, for 'social' reasons[17] in one-fifth of families at the time of referral. Fourteen per cent of families had some kind of contact with the Gardaí. A minority of families were involved with specialist services such as the child psychiatric services, the Community Child Centre, special schools, psychology service and hospitals (see Table 2.20).

TABLE 2.20: OTHER SERVICES INVOLVED WITH FAMILY AT TIME OF REFERRAL (CANN CATEGORY)

Other Services	Percentage (n = 118)
Gardaí	14
School	20
Hospital	3
Child Psychiatry Services	3
Special School	4
CSA Unit	5
Psychology	7
Other	38*

* The 'other' category was composed of family support worker, child care worker, adult psychiatry and day child care.

In some instances, previous contact had taken place between families and the social work service when children were placed 'in care'.[18] In 14 per cent of the 118 CANNs, at least one child was in some form of care outside their birth family. However the majority were in 'informal' placements[19] rather than formal care of the South Eastern Health Board (see Table 2.21).

---

[17] 'Social reasons' include concerns about neglect, learning difficulties, and poor attendance.

[18] By this we mean children already in care when the referral came to SEHB attention rather than those placed in care as a direct response to the referral.

[19] This usually took the form of placement with relative or close family friends, on an informal basis but by agreement with the SEHB.

TABLE 2.21: NUMBER OF CHILDREN IN CARE AT TIME OF REFERRAL OF CHILD ABUSE AND NEGLECT CONCERNS TO SEHB SOCIAL WORK SERVICE

Percentage of Children in Care of:	*% Child Abuse and Neglect Referrals (n = 118)*
SEHB	3
Alternative care	11
Total	14

A final consideration in relation to both categories was the type of response offered by the Health Board to clients within both samples. In addition to further illuminating the nature of referrals in both instances, we also sought to determine if there was a significant difference in the response given to GRSWSs and to CANNs. In relation to the GRSWS category, the data obtained for this part of the study were relatively limited.[20] We used the criterion of whether or not a case file was opened to indicate if a service had been offered,[21] as the opening of a case file would suggest that the initial referral became a 'case' and was allocated to a specific worker for some type of intervention. We found that case files had been open prior to referral on just 16 per cent of 423 clients in the GRSWS category. After referral, case files were newly opened on approximately half of the 423 clients. In order to ascertain the extent of involvement following this, we checked to see if files opened in the GRSWS category were still open after six months.[22] One third were still 'open', indicating a level of contact from the social work service.

---

[20] i.e., information collected by social workers from their May–June referral forms.

[21] According to the practice of the social work department, a case file would be opened if there was any further contact with a client following the initial referral.

[22] This was considered to reflect the provision of a medium term social work or other service. In general where intervention was ceased, case files were closed again. However it must be noted that pressure of work sometimes prevented social workers from doing the work necessary to formally 'close' cases as soon as contact had ceased.

As outlined earlier in relation to CANNs which were notified in May-June, a number of case files were already open. Six months later, two-thirds of the cases in the sample were still 'active', in that a case file was still open.[23] From the findings, it is clear that child abuse and neglect referrals are more likely to receive an ongoing service from the SEHB than GRSWSs. This is evidenced in the fact that two-thirds of cases represented in the CANN category were still open six months later, whereas just one-third of GRSWSs were. While the CANN category is not a direct derivative of the GRSWS category, it may be postulated that at least some of the GRSWS files which were still open after six months related to child abuse and neglect, which featured in one-third of the whole sample of referrals.

This finding coincides with research into community social work services in both the UK (Farmer & Owen, 1995) and Australia (Thorpe, 1994). Both studies found that families are more likely to receive a 'helping service' such as social work involvement if their presenting problems fall within the ambit of child abuse than if they present as disadvantaged or under pressure in other respects. However, the evidence in this research does suggest that the social work service is not necessarily dealing exclusively with child abuse and neglect cases. Other problems, albeit a minority, received some form of ongoing response from the service. Further research would be necessary to explore the particular nature of such referrals before reaching definitive conclusions. However research in the UK has suggested that it is crucial to give attention to referrals other than child abuse, such as behavioural problems in children, parenting difficulties or immature parenting, not least because these are indicative themselves of potential child abuse or neglect (Waterhouse, 1996). This finding relates to a more general feature of the social work service within the health board, in terms of the concentration on child welfare and child abuse issues. It will be explored in more detail at various points throughout the book.

---

[23] As the procedure in the health board was to close case files when intervention had ceased, an open case was taken to indicate some form of continuing contact with the family.

Sections One and Two above have provided a general picture of the range and nature of issues the social work service are presented with. They also highlight the level of difficulties, financially and emotionally, which most persons referred to the service, for whatever reason, seemed to be experiencing. The final section of this chapter considers in particular aspects of the initial intervention of the social work service with CANNs. The aim of this section is to set a clear context for the qualitative study of child protection practices in Phase Two of the research. It provides some useful background data on the process of initial investigation once a child abuse and neglect referral was made to the service.

SECTION THREE: INITIAL STAGE OF INTERVENTION INTO REFERRALS RESULTING IN NOTIFICATION (I.E. CANN CATEGORY)

This section considers briefly the way in which guidelines and procedures were used, the initial investigation and assessment, and the form of planning which took place at the initial stage. Before embarking on this account however, it is useful to consider the identity of alleged perpetrators featured in the 118 CANNs, given that one of the most important factors determining child protection decisions appeared to be whether the alleged perpetrators were closely related to the alleged victims, and whether they lived in close proximity to them. In this study, it was found that over half of alleged perpetrators of abuse or neglect were directly related to the alleged victim. In a quarter of cases, the alleged perpetrator was the mother of the child referred. In a further 14 per cent, the child's father was the alleged perpetrator.[24] Both parents together were considered responsible in a further nine per cent of cases, while parent and cohabitee were considered responsible in a smaller proportion of cases. In summary, at least

---

[24] It is important to note that these are findings for child abuse and neglect as a single category. If the categories were divided into neglect, sexual abuse, physical abuse and emotional abuse, findings from other research suggest that while child neglect is committed by males and females, sexual abuse is primarily committed by alleged male perpetrators. It was beyond the scope of the study to analyse the statistics in this detail.

one parent was alleged responsible for over half of all the child abuse and neglect cases notified. The other alleged perpetrators were primarily persons who had close contact with the child/children, such as siblings, other relatives, family friends or neighbours. Strangers accounted for just 5 per cent of alleged perpetrators of abuse and neglect (see Table 2.22). Furthermore, most alleged perpetrators of abuse or neglect were either living with or in close proximity to the child at the time of referral (see Table 2.23). These findings closely replicate those of British research studies (Cleaver & Freeman, 1995; Thorpe, 1994).

TABLE 2.22: NATURE OF RELATIONSHIP BETWEEN ALLEGED PERPETRATOR AND CHILD

Relationship	Frequency (n = 118)
Mother alone	25
Father and Mother	9
Mother and Cohabitee	2
Parent with other relative	1
Family friend	7
Professional	2
Other	17
Stranger	5
Neighbour	4
Other relative	10
Sibling(s)	3
Father and cohabitee	4
Father alone	14

TABLE 2.23: FORM OF CONTACT BETWEEN ALLEGED PERPETRATOR AND CHILD AT TIME OF REFERRAL

Nature of Relationship	% Referrals (n = 118)
Living with full-time	61
Family friend	11
Professional access	1
Custodial access	1
Other	24

The Use of Child Abuse Guidelines and Procedures

Procedures and guidelines have played an increasingly important role in child protection and welfare services over the past years. In addition to the national child abuse guidelines (*Child Abuse Guidelines: Guidelines on Procedures for the Identification, Investigation and Management of Child Abuse*. Department of Health, 1987) the South Eastern Health Board have developed their own local procedures.[25] They outline the steps to be followed once a referral of abuse or neglect has been made to the social work service. A key recommendations is that, within twenty-four hours, all cases of alleged abuse or neglect should be notified to the Director of Community Care (DCC), with copies sent simultaneously to the Senior Social Worker and the Superintendent Public Health Nurse. Recently published guidelines on the *Notification of Suspected Cases of Child Abuse and Neglect between the Health Boards and the Gardaí* have been introduced and implemented in all health board areas.[26] These guidelines state that the Gardaí should be notified of all suspected cases of abuse and certain cases of neglect which come to the attention of the health board.

All of the procedures cover the possibility of legal intervention where necessary. Not all sections of the *Child Care Act, 1991* had been implemented at the time of the study, and care order proceedings were still being taken under the *Children Act, 1908*.

In our research, we found that the most routine procedure carried out in practice, following referrals of child abuse and neglect, was the notification of reports to the Director of Community Care. This happened in all cases, though only (approximately) 60 per cent of cases were notified within the recommended time-frame of twenty-four hours. A further 25 per cent had been notified within a week of referral. The vast majority of cases referred had been notified within one month of referral (see Table 2.24).

---

[25] *South Eastern Health Board Procedures for the Investigation and Management of Cases of Suspected Child Abuse* (May, 1994).

[26] *Notification of Suspected Cases of Child Abuse Between the Health Boards and the Gardai* (April, 1995).

TABLE 2.24: TIME WITHIN WHICH ALLEGED CHILD ABUSE OR
NEGLECT WAS NOTIFIED TO THE DCC (N = 118)

Time Span	% Notified
Same day	46
Within 24 hours	15
Within 3 days	8
Within one week	18
After one week	5
After two weeks	3
After three weeks	3
After one month	1
Information not available	2
Total	100

Only one-third of child abuse allegations were formally notified to
the Gardaí, principally because the new notification guidelines
had not been fully implemented during the study period. In a further quarter of cases, informal communication took place between
social workers and the Gardaí (see Table 2.25).

TABLE 2.25: NUMBER OF REFERRALS OF CHILD ABUSE OR NEGLECT
REFERRED TO THE GARDAÍ

Were Cases Notified to Gardaí?	% Formal Notification	% Informal Communication
Yes	36	25
No	59	63
Not applicable	-	8
Information not available	6	4
Total	100	100

The *South Eastern Health Board Procedures for the Investigation
and Management of Cases of Suspected Child Abuse* (May, 1994)
stipulates that where children are considered to be in immediate
danger, 'an emergency meeting of the Director of Community
Care, Senior Social Worker and Superintendent Public Health
Nurse is convened'. In 3 per cent of the CANN category such

meetings were convened following notification. Legal interventions resulting in care orders[27] were considered necessary in just 2 per cent of the notifications made. In 8 per cent of cases notified, children were received into care following notification. 'Care' placements comprised full-time care for 4 per cent of cases, private care for 1 per cent, day care for another 2 per cent and alternative care for one case. In the vast majority of cases, however, neither emergency legal procedures nor placement in care were considered necessary (see Table 2.26).

TABLE 2.26: TYPES OF CARE PLACEMENTS USED IN RESPONSE TO CHILD ABUSE OR NEGLECT REFERRALS

	% of Total Sample	% of Children in Care Sample
Statutory care	1	13
Voluntary care	3	37
Day care	1	13
Private care	2	25
Other alternative care*	1	13

* In this case, an alternative care arrangement was made by relatives of a family, as opposed to the SEHB. However, the arrangement was actively supported by the Board.

The issue of social workers and their implementation of guidelines has been analysed in a number of British studies. Corby (1987) for example carried out a study of day-to-day practices of local authority child protection social workers between 1981 and 1985. He found that, while there was a clear-cut guide to investigation of child abuse available to social workers, the practitioners found it difficult to adhere to these procedures. Corby found that this difficulty was related to social workers' unease with carrying out their investigative role. His findings reflects that of Dingwall *et al.* (1983) who found that front line workers tended not to bring cases into the open unless forced to do so, for example, when other agencies became involved. Corby found that an 'informal screening' of cases operated, especially in cases where social workers

---

[27] That is, either a Place of Safety Order or a Fit Person Order, under the *Children Act, 1908*.

were already involved with the family, and therefore tended not to be processed according to the formal guidelines and procedures. He suggests that the reason for this action by social workers was to prevent an over-reaction to families problems or due to fear of the social workers losing control over the situations which they felt they were most suited to dealing with. Pithouse (1987) on the other hand suggests that the reason for social workers not following guidelines to the letter was due to the view that it was only front line social workers who could manage the unpredictable and undefinable nature of their work and their actions evolve from a practice of shared occupational experience with their colleagues. The social workers' perceptions of the guidelines and their interpretations of them are illustrated in the following chapter on social workers' involvement in the child protection system.

Initial Investigation and Assessment

The South Eastern Health Board child abuse procedures recommend that, in addition to completing formal notification procedures, an appointed professional[28] should carry out a preliminary investigation and gather relevant information from other professionals. It is also recommended that the parents and children are seen as soon as possible where appropriate in order to assess the degree of risk to the child (SEHB Procedures, p. 10).

Data from this study show that the persons most often contacted by social workers in the initial stages of investigation were community-based generic professionals. Four key professionals featured significantly: public health nurses were contacted in nearly half of all the cases; teachers and GPs were contacted in one-third of cases, while the Gardaí were contacted in a quarter of cases. In a minority of cases, various other professionals were contacted. These included psychologists, child care workers and family support workers. Most of the persons contacted were able to provide relevant information regarding the different families identified in notifications (Table 2.27).

---

[28] In practice, with few exceptions, this professional was the social worker.

TABLE 2.27: PERSONS CONTACTED REGARDING INITIAL INVESTIGATION

Person Contacted	% of Total	% Found Helpful	% of Those Contacted Found Helpful
General Practitioner	36	30	83
Public Health Nurse	47	42	89
Teacher	35	33	95
Gardaí	26	23	88
Other	22	20	91

A quarter of parents whose children were the subjects of child abuse and neglect notifications had made contact with the South Eastern Health Board themselves, therefore the question of when they were contacted in relation to the initial investigation is not applicable. Otherwise, most parents were contacted at some stage during the initial investigation. Almost 20 per cent had been contacted within a day of the initial referral. By the end of the first week, 36 per cent had been contacted and this figure had risen to nearly 50 per cent by the end of the first month. Including the parents who made contact themselves (25 per cent), approximately three-quarters of parents had been made aware of the notifications within one month of the reports having been made. Allowing for the fact that some information was unavailable, the data suggest that at least 12 per cent of all parents were not contacted at all about the child abuse and neglect concerns relating to their family (Table 2.28).

The South Eastern Health Board procedures also recommend that children are seen as soon as possible to assess possible risk. Children were seen at some stage in nearly three-quarters of cases notified.

- A quarter of children were seen the day concerns were raised;

- A further quarter were seen within a week of referral;

- The majority of children seen were visited within a month;

- Over a quarter of children who were 'notified' were not seen at all by a social worker or other professional at the initial investigative stage (see Table 2.29).

TABLE 2.28: TIME SPAN WITHIN WHICH PARENTS WERE CONTACTED REGARDING THE ABUSE AND NEGLECT CONCERN

Time-Span within which Parents were Contacted	*% Referrals (n = 118)*
Day concerns were raised	16
Within 24 hours	3
Within three days	4
Within a week	12
Within a month	14
Within three months	5
Not at all	12
Not applicable	25
Missing information	9
Total	100

TABLE 2.29: WHO SAW CHILDREN TO ASSESS LEVEL OF RISK FOLLOWING REFERRAL OF CHILD ABUSE OR NEGLECT

Professional	*% of All CANNs (n = 118)*	*% of Children Who Were Seen to Assess Risk (n = 89)*
Social Worker alone	36	48
Social Worker/GP	1	1
Social Worker/PHN	1	1
Social Worker/Child Care Worker	2	3
PHN alone	6	8
PHN/Area Medical Officer	1	1
Area Medical Officer alone	1	1
Child Care Worker alone	2	3
General Practitioner alone	3	4
Other	17	23
Not Seen at All	27	-
Information Not Available	3	4

Children were most often seen for initial risk assessment by a social worker. This happened in a over a third of cases notified. In a few instances, children were seen jointly by a social worker with another professional. Public health nurses were also involved in initial risk assessment, either individually or with another professional. A smaller number of children were initially seen by a general practitioner, child care worker or Area Medical Officer (AMO). Other professionals who saw children for risk assessment in the initial stages of investigation included hospital doctors, teachers or specialist professionals.

In some instances, children required further specialist assessment, or validation, particularly when the allegations concerned sexual and physical abuse. Further assessment was deemed necessary in nearly half of the notified cases. The agency which carried out the largest proportion of such assessments was the Community Child Centre at Waterford Regional Hospital. Assessments by psychologists also occurred in a number of cases. A range of medical examinations was also carried out in a small percentage of cases, by general practitioners and hospital doctors. In addition, a small number of behavioural and educational assessments were carried out (see Table 2.30).

TABLE 2.30: FURTHER CHILD ASSESSMENTS CARRIED OUT IN RESPONSE TO ALLEGATIONS OF ABUSE OR NEGLECT

Form of Assessment	% of Total (n=118)	% of all those Assessed (n=50)*
CSA Unit	20	48
CSA/Other Assessment	1	2
CSA/Psychology	1	2
Medical GP	3	7
Medical CSA	2	5
Medical Hospital	2	5
Psychological	10	24
Psychological/Other	1	2
Other	4	10
Not applicable	56**	-
Information not available	2	-

* 42 per cent of total sample.

** no assessment took place in those cases.

In summary, this study found that social workers almost always routinely notified child abuse and neglect reports to the Director of Community Care, though not always within the recommended time scale of twenty-four hours. Notifications to Gardaí took place on a smaller scale at that particular time, though this situation is likely to have changed with firmer implementation of the guidelines for *Notification of Cases of Suspected Child Abuse Between the Health Boards and the Gardaí*. Legal procedures were used in very few cases. The investigation and assessment of child abuse and neglect was carried out by a range of professionals, who co-operated with each other by providing information, and, in some cases, carrying out further assessment. The central responsibility for co-ordination of the process was carried by social workers. Most parents of the children concerned in the notifications were seen early in the investigation, though 12 per cent were not contacted at all. Likewise, most children were seen by a professional in the very early stages, though one-quarter were not seen at all. More detailed assessments and medical examinations on notified children were carried out by a variety of professionals, depending on the individual case.

In general, the child abuse procedures which shape the initial response of the social work service to a referral of suspected child abuse and neglect appear to have been applied with a certain level of flexibility, as in the case of guidelines and notifications discussed in the previous section. The most notable discrepancies between recommended procedure and action by social worker include the fact that over 10 per cent of parents were not made aware of the notifications at any point in the initial stage, and almost a quarter of children were not seen at this stage either. There are a number of possibilities for this lack of strict adherence to procedures. As outlined earlier in relation to guidelines, there are a number of different arguments as to why set procedures may not be followed to the letter by social workers (Pithouse, 1987; Corby, 1986; Dingwall *et al.*, 1983). The methodology used in the present research does not lend itself to making postulations as to the reason for lack of adherence to procedures. However, findings from Phase Two will help to illuminate the kind of issues raised for social workers and other professionals in relation to official policy and procedures.

The initial investigative stage consists primarily of making the necessary notifications, contacting the relevant professionals, and making direct contact with the children and their families. Once sufficient information has been gathered and an assessment made, the next logical stage in the process of intervention was the initial planning phase. Findings relating to how this evolved in relation to the CANN category are provided in the following section.

Initial Planning Stage

In our research we found that planning at this initial stage took one of two paths: (1) formal planning, which took place most frequently in the form of a case conference; and (2) informal planning between workers and their managers, or between the social work service and other professionals. Informal planning was the most frequently used form of planning in relation to child abuse and neglect notifications.

Beginning with Case Conferences, we found that they were allocated a central role in both the initial investigation and ongoing management of child abuse and neglect cases. The South Eastern Health Board procedures suggest that a case conference will be held in the following circumstances:

- when initial information or assessment has established that there is significant harm or risk to a child, e.g. physical abuse, sexual abuse, neglect or emotional abuse;

- where it is necessary to formulate a child protection plan and there is a need for sharing of information and decisions on an inter-disciplinary and/or inter-agency nature;

- where initial assessment indicates that there is a need to consider legal action;

- when a child who was a subject of alleged abuse is being discharged from care, with a view to any relevant issues being discussed.

In 25 per cent of the CANN category, case conferences were held, at some point in the initial period, to discuss the child abuse and neglect notifications which were made during the study period. Of those, a minority were emergency conferences which took place immediately or shortly after the notification of alleged abuse or neglect was made. The majority of case conferences were held following the initial investigation, in order to plan ongoing intervention: one-third (36 per cent) were held within a month of the notification and a further 44 per cent were held within three months (see Table 2.31).

TABLE 2.31: WHEN WERE CASE CONFERENCES HELD?

Time Span	% of Total (n = 118)	% of Case Conferences (n = 30)
Within a week	1	4
One week – one month	9	36
One – three months	11	44
Three – four months	3	12
No Case Conference held	75	-
Information not available	1	4
Total	100	100

The South Eastern Health Board child abuse procedures describe the principal aim of the case conference as the bringing together of 'relevant professionals involved with the particular child so that they can pool information about the child and his or her circumstances, so as to develop a clearer picture of the risks to the child' (South Eastern Health Board procedures, p. 12). Table 2.32 indicates which professionals normally attended case conferences. The most regular attendees were Health Board personnel including the Senior Area Medical Officers, or the Director of Community Care, the Senior Social Workers or Team Leaders, social workers, the public health nurses with their Superintendent or Seniors. Other than Health Board personnel, the Gardaí were the most regular attendees at case conferences, at over 40 per cent. Teachers attended almost a third of all case conferences held and general practitioners attended in nearly a quarter of cases. These figures suggest community services not only play a significant role in the identification and referral of child abuse and neglect but also in on-going case planning. The range of other professionals attending case conferences varied with different cases. For example, a professional from the Community Child Centre usually attended if the child or children involved had attended their unit for validation. Parental attendance at the case conference was extremely low at 4 per cent. In two cases, parents attended for part of the discussion and, in another two instances, parents attended for feedback.

TABLE 2.32: WHO ATTENDED CASE CONFERENCES

	% Yes	% No	% Do Not Know
Senior Area Medical Officer/DCC	85	7	8
Senior Social Worker/Team Leader	96	-	4
Social Worker	92	-	8
Community Care Worker	4	88	8
Public Health Nurse	85	7	8
Senior Public Health Nurse	85	7	8
GP	24	68	8
Gardaí	41	51	8
Teacher	31	61	8
Family Support Worker	4	88	8
CSA Social Worker	17	74	8
Other Professionals	31	61	8
Parents	4	88	8

As outlined above, in 25 per cent of cases notified, a case conference was held to plan intervention into families where a notification of suspected abuse or neglect had been made. As the South Eastern Health Board guidelines emphasise the importance of drawing up a child protection plan in all cases it is important to consider the form of planning which took place in the remainder of the cases represented in the CANNs. The SEHB Procedures provide a specially designed 'child protection plan' for this purpose. However we found no evidence of this being in use at the time of the study. Apart from case conference minutes, case records showed no other evidence that the 'formal' planning suggested in the procedures actually took place.

Most files showed that some type of informal planning took place between social workers and other persons involved, either through telephone contact or face-to-face office meetings between relevant personnel. Such informal contact was most likely to occur between social workers and the Gardaí. In approximately one-quarter of files examined, no evidence was found to suggest that either a formal or informal planning meeting was held (see Table 2.33).

TABLE 2.33: FORM OF CHILD PROTECTION PLAN DRAWN UP IN RESPONSE TO CHILD ABUSE AND NEGLECT REFERRALS

Context of Plan	*% Cases (n = 18)*
At Case Conference	25
At Planning Meeting	18
Plan drawn up informally	25
No plan	28
Information missing	4
Total	100

The level of involvement of both professionals and parents in the construction of such plans for intervention was explored. Social workers, in consultation with their supervisors, were particularly active in, and central to, case planning. Additionally, the community-based services such as public health nurses, the Gardaí, schools and, to a lesser extent, GPs, were involved in both formal and informal planning meetings. Other professionals included community child care workers, youth workers, residential child care workers and family support workers. It would appear that planning meetings were likely to be held where professionals other than social workers were involved in the case. There was a significantly low level of involvement of parents involved in the actual construction of plans,[29] though they do appear to have been

---

[29] Though they were likely to be informed of the content of the constructed plan.

more involved in formal or informal planning meetings than case conferences.

The range of decisions made at such meetings varied considerably. The nature and gravity of the child abuse concerns obviously determined the recommendations made, which included, for example, placement of a child in care, assessment at the Community Child Centre, Garda involvement or social work involvement, such as 'follow-up' or 'monitoring'.

In summary, case records indicate that parental involvement in planning interventions remained at a fairly low level at the initial stage of intervention by the social work service. Very few parents attended any part of a case conference and only a minority were involved in the construction of child protection plans relating to their families.

Although there was little explicit evidence of formal child protection plans having been agreed, case records indicate that some level of planning takes place in most cases. It was generally informal and was most likely to occur where at least one professional other than the social worker was involved. Official child protection plan forms were not used in any of the cases examined. When plans were made, they tended to be short term, such as 'Gardaí to visit', or non-specific, such as 'social worker to monitor'. It is likely that the key practitioners involved in each case had a sound knowledge of the framework within which they were working, but the absence of explicit written plans meant that information was not readily accessible in the absence of the worker involved. The nature of child care planning is explored in more detail in the following chapter which begins a more in-depth analysis of a sample of notified cases (Phase Two).

The data also suggest that, apart from the social workers, a broad range of professionals were involved with the families in relation to some aspect of the case from the initial point. Once again, community-based 'generic' services (public health nurses, teachers, Gardaí, GPs) continued to play a significant role, and regularly attended case conferences. Despite a high level of involvement by other professionals, however, social workers appeared to carry the central responsibility for planning of interventions and the actual ongoing work with families. Other professionals worked with, rather than instead of, social workers, and carried out quite specific work. In contrast, social workers carried out a broader range of tasks, encompassing a general monitoring and supportive role.

CONCLUSION

The aim of this chapter has been two-fold. Firstly, it aimed to provide a broad overview of the nature of work carried out by the social work service and the key characteristics of persons referred to the service from both GRSWS and CANN categories. Secondly, we aimed to consider more specifically the nature of intervention into child abuse and neglect cases which were notified following referral. The findings from this section form the basis on which a more qualitative analysis of child protection practices was carried out in Phase Two of the study, where 18 out of the 118 CANN category are considered in depth.

Findings from Section One and Two above suggest that persons referred to the social work service, either for general reasons or specific child abuse and neglect concerns, are likely to be suffering both financial and material pressures as well as significant family or personal difficulties. Despite the fact that both groups appeared to experience significant socio-economic and emotional stresses, it was found to be far more likely that clients referred in relation to child abuse and neglect would receive an ongoing service than those involved in general referrals. This seems to coincide with findings from social services areas in the UK, as well as health boards in Ireland, where the focus of community social work has become more and more defined within child protection and welfare terms, rather than within a broader concept of personal or family need. As this finding relates to the nature of the community care social work service in general, we will examine its implications in a more general sense in our final chapter, which explores a range of aspects of the overall 'system'.

Findings from Section Two also highlight the dependence of the social work service on professionals and lay persons in the community to bring individuals and families to their attention. The most significant source of referral to the social work service of the SEHB was found to be generic professionals such as teachers,

GPs, Gardaí and public health nurses. Analysis of data from Section Three confirms the central role of professionals within the child welfare and protection system from the initial stages of intervention. Throughout the findings, however, it is clear that social workers are the front line personnel in the process and, while other professionals play a key role, this tends to be alongside social workers rather than instead of them. Section Three, for example, illuminates the key responsibility social workers carry for the notification and investigation of child abuse. This is endorsed in both local and national procedures and guidelines. It shows that social workers carried out their statutory role with a certain amount of discretion, especially in terms of when notifications were made and of deciding whether parents and children were seen. While the procedures also recommend a formal planning meeting to be held to plan interventions, the way in which plans were constructed was found to be primarily informal, except in the cases where a case conference was held. We have suggested in this chapter that the relationship between formal procedures and actual practice is a complex one. Findings from Phase Two will illuminate social workers' and other professionals' perceptions of such guides for practice. This will allow for a fuller discussion in later stages of the book.

Overall, Phase One findings have provided a broad profile of the nature of the social work service, key characteristics of persons referred to the service, and the central role a range of other professionals and persons in the community play in its successful operation. We have been able to place the particular child abuse and neglect cases (CANNs) within this context and make some preliminary comparison between the two categories (GRSWSs & CANNs) in order to gauge the place of CANNs within the overall service. We have also provided some preliminary findings in relation to the initial investigation of CANNs which provide the basis on which Phase Two was carried out.

The remainder of this book focuses on the findings from Phase Two. As outlined above, the two phases are not mutually exclusive; thus, where relevant, Phase One findings are used to illuminate or complement the qualitative findings represented in Phase Two.

CHAPTER THREE

SOCIAL WORK INVOLVEMENT IN THE CHILD PROTECTION PROCESS: FROM INITIAL INVESTIGATION TO ON-GOING MANAGEMENT OF CASES

INTRODUCTION: SOCIAL WORKERS' ROLE WITHIN THE CHILD PROTECTION SYSTEM[1]

Because of the central position allocated to social workers under the child abuse guidelines, all those who had been involved in the eighteen cases represented in the research were interviewed, irrespective of the level of their current involvement. All of the cases had an allocated social worker, who had been nominated as the 'key' worker in most instances. In a minority of situations, this key role was held by another practitioner. For example, in one instance, parents had refused access to the Health Board after the initial investigation and the general practitioner, who was acceptable to the family, had agreed with the Health Board to adopt the central child protection role. There were three more instances in which social workers had little to no involvement, though the cases were still regarded as active. In one of those, the lack of contact was again due to parental resistance, and in two it was because the social worker had held that position for only five months and, due to pressure of other work, had not yet met the families concerned. However even in those instances where social workers were not actively involved in the actual cases, they were still identified as the central professionals within the child abuse

---

[1] As the methodology section in Chapter One has outlined, Phase Two of the study focused on a sample of eighteen child abuse cases selected from the total number notified in May/June 1995.

system[2] This was reflected in interviews with both social workers themselves and with other professionals.

Due to the primacy of the social work role within the overall child protection system, the views and perceptions of social workers are represented throughout the remaining chapters of the book, in relation to their own role, relations with other professionals, involvement with parents and their views on the child protection system in general. In this chapter, we begin this analysis by focusing on two key areas particular to social work: social workers and the initial stages of intervention (Section One); and the process of ongoing management of cases by the social work team following the investigative period (Section Two). More specifically, in Section One, as the actual 'mechanics' of the investigative stage have already been analysed in Phase One findings detailed in Chapter Four, the focus will be on the procedures for notification of child abuse and neglect, the construction and review of plans and the involvement of clients at this early stage of intervention. Section Two then considers the ongoing process of the case. In this analysis we concentrate on social workers' views of progress in the cases and their relationship with their clients over the six month period, their perceptions of the factors which affected the ongoing management of the cases, and their measurement of the adequacy of the service the social work service within the Health Board offered to their clients.

SECTION ONE: SOCIAL WORKERS' PERCEPTIONS OF THE INITIAL STAGES OF INTERVENTION

Findings in Chapter Two demonstrated that referrals of child abuse and neglect cases came from a range of sources including professionals, parents, concerned neighbours or other members of the public. However, once referred, in the vast majority of cases it was a social worker who made the notification of child abuse or neglect to the DCC, as stipulated in the SEHB *Procedures for Investigation and Management of Child Abuse and Neglect*. Notifications were processed through the medium of a Notification

---

[2] This will be illuminated throughout the book.

Meeting, which was held once weekly in most instances.[3] The stated purpose of the meetings was to discuss new notifications and give guidelines as to the appropriate action to be taken. Previous notifications were also reviewed if there were any outstanding questions to be answered. The meetings were attended in each community care area by the Director of Community Care or a delegated Area Medical Officer, Social Work Managers and Senior Public Health Nurses. Social workers themselves did not attend the meetings in any area but usually submitted a completed child abuse notification form accompanied by a preliminary report on the alleged child abuse or neglect.

Analysis of data from both Phase One and Phase Two indicates that feedback from the Child Abuse Notification Meetings tended to fall into three main categories:

- direction as to which personnel should be notified;

- direction as to whether a case conference is necessary;

- direction as to what action should be taken next by the social worker.

The holding of case conferences was suggested in one-fifth of all the child abuse notifications examined in Phase One. A range of suggestions for further action by social workers were made, for example, if the notification concerned child sexual abuse, referral to the Community Child Centre in Waterford was usually recommended. Other suggestions from the meetings included requests for more detailed reports, advice to the social workers to 'monitor and support' and 'visit' families. Social workers were frequently requested to link with other professionals, most often public health nurses, or to make a referral to another service, most often the psychology service. The social workers' role as front line agents in child protection work is evident in these recommendations. Furthermore, not only are social workers most often the person requested to take the preliminary action, but it seems that, in many cases, there was a tendency for the meetings to en-

---

[3] In one of the four community care areas, this meeting occurred less frequently at the time of the study but it was indicated that there were plans to increase their frequency in the near future.

dorse the recommendations already made by the social worker in
the preliminary report.

The social workers who were interviewed in Phase Two of the
study reflected a generally positive attitude to the introduction of
Child Abuse Notification Meetings. Many of the social workers
interviewed considered the meetings to 'give a sense of shared responsibility for the case'. For example, one worker commented
that she felt they were important: 'if you have a case where allegations come in, at least it's not the front line workers making all
the decisions'. Another commented that the meetings 'were good
for sharing ideas and responsibility' but added that 'it can be difficult if you do not agree with all the decisions being made'. The
meetings were also considered by many of the social workers to be
useful for creating awareness amongst management of the level
and nature of the work that was being done and in highlighting
any gaps in it: 'It's a good way of letting management know what
individual social workers are dealing with . . . it can show a short
fall in the service'. Others found that the meetings provided indicators of the level of work in progress where 'previously nobody
knew how much work was being done'. Some practitioners saw
the meetings as useful for keeping cases 'on the boil'. Another
worker suggested that 'the meetings keep the case alive . . . they
look for reports and reviews and this keeps things going'.

However deficits were also identified in the notification meeting process. The most prevalent of these were limited participation of social workers in the notification meetings, a dissatisfaction with the form of feedback received, and a scepticism about
the real usefulness of the meetings.

Several social workers expressed the view that they themselves should have more active participation in the meetings
which were described by one worker as 'an anonymous entity'. It
was suggested that 'sometimes decisions are made on too little
information and it would be more useful if the worker was present
to give the detail and answer questions'. Some social workers
were critical of the practice of giving feedback on official forms,
and were dissatisfied with having to 'rely on your supervisor to
inform you of the decisions of the meeting'. Another worker commented that 'sending forms is not real communication . . . it just

makes you feel that you are covered'. Concern was also expressed by the social workers about the purpose of the meetings. A worry was expressed that they were becoming 'procedure for procedure's sake', or 'ends in themselves'. The ability of the meetings to realistically address complex issues was questioned by one social worker: 'I often get a sense that they just rubber stamp the recommondations the social workers make on the preliminary report' and another worker commented:

> . . . while they are a good thing . . . sometimes you get unrealistic requests for stuff, like weekly reports . . . those kinds of things just aren't on if you are loaded down with work.

In summary, Child Abuse Notification Meetings were primarily used to give advice about the appropriate response to child abuse reports and to endorse social work decisions. Social workers themselves generally found them helpful but expressed some concern about how the meetings were conducted and about what their purpose was. A number of workers expressed the view that they should have the opportunity to attend the meetings themselves, especially where they were notifying cases which were particularly complicated or detailed.

CHILD PROTECTION PLANS

Following the child abuse notification meetings and initial investigative action, the next stage in the processing of child abuse allegations was found to be the construction of a child protection plan. The South Eastern Health Board procedures contain an official form to be used in outlining the planned intervention in all open cases of alleged child abuse and neglect. As outlined in Chapter Two, such forms were not in operation at the time of the study; therefore it was not possible to evaluate their use.

However, despite the fact that official procedure was not followed in relation to child protection plans, the data gathered, from case files in the CANN category in Phase One, and in interviews with social workers in Phase Two, suggests that plans for intervention were made along three possible paths, which were:

- the child abuse notification meetings

- case conferences, and

- through informal consultation with Social Work Managers and/or other professionals involved.

The descriptions of child protection plans in the eighteen sample cases in Phase Two reflect this pattern. Plans included notification to the Gardaí, referral to the Community Child Centre in cases of child sexual abuse (recommended in eight out of the eighteen sample cases), referral to other services and liaison with other professionals. However, in the majority of cases the plans consisted of action by the social workers themselves. The predominant tasks outlined were:

- to visit parents and address the child protection concerns;

- to monitor the family;

- to offer support to the family and children;

- to carry out tasks such as ensuring that abusing parents did not have access to children; and

- to do protection work with a child or children.

In seven of the sample cases, various forms of alternative care were either actively sought or considered. One child was placed in emergency care, another in a foster home and a third in a children's home while placements were sought for his siblings. Day fostering and care with relatives were considered for other children, and, in two cases, care proceedings were postponed on condition that agreed work was carried out.

Child protection plans were normally recorded in either case conference minutes, or on the notification forms, but were not otherwise put in writing. Our observations from Phase One, where we found that plans were not clearly visible in the case records, prompted us to ask the social workers if they would favour the idea of putting child protection plans in writing, separately from case records, case conference minutes or other reports, and having them circulated to all members of the child protection network. The majority of social workers interviewed considered that separate, written child protection plans would be useful. It was suggested that:

> . . . a formal plan would mean there would have to be more consultation than what is just sent down from the notification meetings . . .

> . . . other professionals would know better what was going on and see who is doing what . . .

and

> . . . you're more likely to refer back to a formal plan than going to case conference minutes to check a decision . . .

Some reservations were expressed about the time that would be required to draw up plans in writing 'with our present caseloads' and a minority of social workers were unsure about the efficacy of having written case plans, particularly if they were the only professionals involved, or if circumstances in the case were continually changing. The majority view, however, favoured the introduction of separate, written plans which would be sent to all the nominated personnel.

Despite the absence of formal child protection plans, informal strategies for action were found to have existed in all the sample cases. The majority of plans were made either directly from the recommendations of Child Abuse Notification Meetings, or as a result of consultation with social work managers. In three of the cases, the social workers constructed the plans themselves. In another case the social worker did not know the context in which the plan had been made, as she was not involved at the time of the initial investigation.

In all but one case, the social worker was identified as the key person to actually carry out or co-ordinate the child protection plan. The exception was where a family refused contact with the Board and the general practitioner was delegated the role of 'case manager' at a case conference. In eleven out of the eighteen cases, the social worker was the only professional designated to carry out the plan, though other professionals would have had some type of involvement. In other cases, the nominated persons included public health nurses, psychologists, child care workers, and the Community Child Centre. A garda, a teacher and a foster parent were also allocated particular roles in three separate cases. In all of these situations, overall responsibility for co-ordination of the case lay with the social worker involved.

In the majority of the cases examined, there was evidence that, in most instances, the greater part of the initial child protection plans were followed. There were some exceptions to this, one being where the social worker was no longer directly involved and not in a position to comment, and the other where the recommendation for day care could not be implemented due to the unavailability of a placement. In two cases, the social worker had not met the families involved but assumed that the original plan was in operation. The situations where child protection plans were only partially followed were primarily linked to instances where referrals to particular services were arranged and parents refused to attend, or where the social workers had a 'lack of time to visit regularly'.

Two-thirds of child protection plans (twelve) in the sample had been reviewed since their construction, and reviews were reported to have been due to take place in most of the other cases. In two cases, plans had not been modified in the previous six months because the social workers had not had time to visit the families, and, in a third, delay in involving a child care worker had temporarily halted progress. Approximately half of the reviews were conducted in a formal inter-professional context, and others at supervision. In three cases, the social workers reported that they constantly reviewed the cases themselves.

Apart from case conferences which were held when serious concerns arose, there did not appear to be a consistent rationale which determined whether cases were reviewed or not. In only one case was a system set up whereby the child protection plan was reviewed formally on a regular monthly basis. The most consistent reasons for not reviewing cases appeared to be either where the social worker had very little or no contact with the family, or where the social worker intended to visit but did not have time to do so. The impetus for review appeared to be primarily left to the discretion of the social worker, who had the responsibility to either set up a formal review or seek an informal meeting.

To summarise, it appears that child protection plans were made in a number of different ways, mostly informally, but in most cases, some form of plan was found to have existed. Formal written plans were not used in any of the cases though most social workers favoured this idea. The child protection plans which were in existence were almost always quite short-term and were reviewed at least once as the case progressed over the six months which this study covered. Social workers themselves seemed to instigate reviews. This usually happened when there was a new social worker in the case or circumstances in the case had changed dramatically. Reviews were therefore unlikely to occur unless the individual social worker made the decision to do so. This finding points to the need for a more formal and regular system of review of open child protection cases which does not rely on the discretion of the individual social worker.

Once a plan was constructed, the next stage was the ongoing management of the case and the implementation of the plans. In Section Two, we explore certain areas of the ongoing process from the social workers' perspective. As outlined earlier, as social workers are such an integral part of the child protection system, their views are also recorded throughout the following chapters. In this section we focus on a) social workers views as regards progress in the case over the time of their involvement,[4] b) the factors which affected, either positively or negatively, their ongoing management of the case, and c) their view as to the adequacy of the service offered to the clients by the social work service.

SECTION TWO: PROCESS OF ONGOING CASE MANAGEMENT FROM THE SOCIAL WORKERS' PERSPECTIVE

A) Progress in Child Protection Cases

Social workers were asked to give their perceptions of 'progress' in the sample cases. Definitions of progress were divided into three

---

[4] Phase Two of the study took place over February–March 1996, therefore cases had been open for at least eight to nine months at this stage.

categories: (1) progress for the child; (2) progress for the family in relation to the child protection concern; and (3) progress in interventions in the family regarding issues other than the reason for referral. 'Progress' and 'outcomes' in child protection cases are notoriously difficult to measure (Cheetham, Fuller, McIvor & Petch, 1992) and it is particularly difficult to distinguish natural developments within the family situation from those which were brought about by professional interventions. For this reason, social workers rarely gave a 'yes' or 'no' answer on the concept of progress. Rather, certain factors were identified as illustrating progress, while others were considered indicative of no progress. In three cases, where there had been no social work involvement from the time of referral, no progress at all was identified. In four other situations, definite progress was identified in relation to all aspects of the case. However in the remainder of the cases, there were mixed views, where progress was deemed to have occurred in some areas but not in others.

In one of the cases, where physical and sexual abuse by the mother's partner had been alleged, progress was identified by virtue of the fact that:

> . . . the abusing parent is gone as a response to the investigation and the children and their mother are a lot more relaxed . . . the mother is more open to the possibility that the abuse may have been caused by her partner . . . the home maker works like a family friend and is very successful . . . there is a general marked improvement.

In this case, progress at three levels is identified: diminished risk for the children since the abuser left the home (progress for the child), the mother's increased ability to protect the children once she accepted that her partner was the perpetrator (progress for the family in relation to the child abuse allegation), and progress related to more general coping reflected in the successful interventions of the home maker (progress for the family more generally).

In another case, progress was reported because:

> . . . the girls have returned home, the level of aggression in the home has been reduced and there have been no further

allegations . . . also the mother and the children attended the Child and Family Centre for counselling.

Progress is here defined more narrowly in terms of protection and support for the children. Likewise another social worker defined progress in terms of child protection and welfare:

> There have been a number of layers of progress in this case . . . the assessment has been carried out by the unit, the mother has co-operated with the Health Board, the child has transferred from an adult to an adolescents' hostel, has got a job . . . she eventually returned home and relations are better at home now.

The most frequent response by the social workers was in terms of 'mixed progress' in the cases. Some of the responses represented an assessment of progress in relation to both the child's needs and the wider family support needs. One social worker for example reported that, at one level,

> . . . there is progress as the father and child are no longer sleeping in the same bed . . . now the child has her own room . . . but the housing continues to be a big issue . . . there is no electricity, running water . . . the council have got involved but have been slow to get services in . . . the mother has separated her welfare payments . . . regarding the child sexual abuse, there are no grounds to question it further due to insufficient information.

In some other cases, the 'mixed' progress was defined more narrowly in terms of progress for the child and progress for the parents in direct relation to the child abuse concern, but not in relation to other aspects of their welfare. In the following example, a child had run away and alleged that her father had sexually abused her. She later returned home, but her social worker was unsure if her emotional state was any better than previously:

> Yes, there has been progress regarding the child . . . she will now discuss issues about home and school. But I don't think she is any happier than she was initially . . . she had pressed for the return home but now is less happy again . . . she will not discuss the child sexual abuse, resists all at-

tempts to bring it up. The day fostering is positive, gives support to the father . . . a break . . . the girls benefit from the care of their aunt, it provides structure. Regarding protection, the child is more able to discuss things openly, except the child sexual abuse.

In a physical abuse case, a child whose parents were separated had been received into emergency care as a result of an assault by her father, with whom she lived. She had subsequently returned home, but had later gone to live with her mother after a second incident. The social worker was undecided about how far the Health Board interventions had progressed the case and was dubious about overall improvements in their family relationships and general well-being:

From the beginning it was a mistake that the child went home without the court imposing any conditions . . . the progress is that the child has been able to separate from her father so it has changed for the better . . . but I can't see her being able to have a relationship with everyone in the family because the father is inclined to polarise the family relationships. The father himself won't join in the family therapy . . . progress with him is very slow.

These examples highlight the difficulty in defining progress. While all the respondents gave us detailed and thoughtful responses, the majority of social workers based their view of progress primarily on the child protection issues. Social workers were less likely to assess progress within the broader ambit of progress for the family in relation to issues other than child protection, and those who did seemed to report less successful accounts of progress.

B) Factors Affecting the Management of Cases

Social workers were asked to identify the factors which were considered by them to have affected the on-going management of the cases in our sample. Both negative and positive factors were considered. The factor most frequently mentioned was supervision by Senior Social Workers and Team Leaders. Other factors included the relationship between the worker and the family, relationships with other professionals, pressure of work, structural factors and some personal issues. A representation of the workers' comments and views are recorded below.

Social Work Supervision

Supervision featured as one of the most significant factors identified by the social workers affecting the ongoing management of child abuse cases. This included both formal and informal supervision.

It was found that there was a variation in the level of formal supervision given to the social workers in our sample. Six of the respondents reported that they had supervision sessions at least once monthly. Six others said they did not get formal supervision at all, and, in the remaining cases, social workers said they had supervision, on average, every two to three months.

There were mixed views about the level and quality of formal supervision received by the social workers, the majority of them being quite critical. One worker, who was new, was dissatisfied when interviewed in March:

> Since November, I have had two supervision sessions and that has been by two different people . . . it's not enough, you need it – especially if you are new.

Another conceded that while she had supervision fairly regularly, she had 'so many cases to get through, this one rarely comes up'. Another was critical that it was left to individuals to suggest the agenda for supervision:

> . . . this is not the best way, it leaves the responsibility of bringing issues to supervision purely on the social worker, who shouldn't be making decisions on their own.

A further difficulty identified was the way supervision time was limited to discussing urgent matters:

> . . . it would be good to have time to discuss things in depth rather than deciding what you will do next . . . it would be great if you had the time to go through all of the cases but this is impossible at the moment.

The desire to use supervision to explore case plans, tease out perspectives and question current interventions was expressed by a number of workers. One worker commented that:

> I need to discuss my work in detail . . . and to plan . . . but also you need to be challenged about what you are doing . . . at no stage in this case was I challenged about my planning or management of the case by my supervisor . . . it would have been really helpful if I had been.

A small number of social workers, however, were generally satisfied with the level of formal supervision that they were receiving. One worker reported that she got:

> . . . regular supervision . . . but it is usually on demand rather than regular . . . I ask for it as often as I need it. The Team Leader and Senior Social Worker are very busy and sometimes you need to just go with things, not to put pressure on them . . . but you know they are there to consult with . . . they are very approachable.

Another social worker commented:

> I get supervision about every six to eight weeks, and I think this is fine . . . there is plenty of scope for informal supervision in between . . . both kinds are helpful and good.

Although the level and quality of formal supervision was deemed unsatisfactory in the majority of instances, all respondents reported that they got satisfactory and regular 'informal' supervision, which took the form of consultations with the Senior Social Worker or Team Leader when the need arose to discuss a case. Most social workers reported easy access to their Social Work Managers. One social worker, for example, pointed out:

> Supervision is often arranged and then has to be postponed because something has come up either for me or for the Senior . . . but I've got a lot of informal supervision on it . . . this is really helpful . . . I get any amount of informal support I need.

Another worker commented:

> Supervision is irregular . . . about four times a year, but my Senior is always available and approachable . . . the effect of informal supervision has been great.

We went on to ask social workers about the effect of supervision on the medium to long-term management of child abuse cases. As so much supervision appears to be given on an informal basis, the effects of both formal and informal supervision on cases were considered simultaneously.

In five out of the eighteen cases, social workers claimed that supervision had no effect on the management of their cases. Most social workers, however, suggested a variety of positive outcomes of supervision.[5] For example it was considered to be a forum for shared responsibility:

> Supervision has meant shared responsibility . . . like the decision to send the child home . . . it gives you back up, and it helps to be told that you have not made a hames of things.

It was also considered useful in keeping things moving:

> Supervision helped speed things up and emphasised when tasks were urgent and needed to be done with whatever discipline is involved . . . it gives an overall view of what needs to be done generally . . .

While another pointed out:

> . . . supervision has made things happen . . . and it lets the social worker feel supported. It also gives a chance to discuss and make contingency plans and gives you time out . . . it's hard to think of the future when you're busy.

Supervision was particularly valued where it helped to deal with complications or difficult issues in the case. As one worker commented:

---

[5] Though most social workers stipulated that they meant informal supervision here.

> This is a complex case and there is a need to check out the
> social work role . . . it's important to consult about the di-
> rection of the work and to provide a forum for constant re-
> view of the case.

A number of workers also recognised the personal support provided by supervision:

> It's helpful to talk . . . to off-load worries and doubts . . .
> draw bottom lines and compare gut feelings.

*Relationships between Social Workers and Families in Child Abuse
Cases*

Most social workers identified the nature of the relationship they
had with the family as affecting the progress of the case – either
positively or negatively. In the majority of cases, the social workers had managed to secure good relationships with families, despite the sometimes very fraught nature of their initial contact.
The level of co-operation from parents was perceived as a very
strong determining factor in the management of ongoing work. In
certain cases, this was influenced by extraneous factors, such as
the client's understanding that it was in their own interests to
work with the Health Board. For example, in a situation involving
a conflict over custody, the social worker was aware that 'the father has a clear agenda in co-operating with me, and has been
advised to do so by his solicitor'. She considered that this had
significantly and positively influenced her ability to work with the
child involved. In another instance, where the family actively re-
sisted the Health Board's involvement and would only work
through their general practitioner, the social worker reported that
'parental lack of involvement and response to professional involvement has had a huge impact on the case'. A different example was given by another worker of where 'Parents' refusal to
meet (the social worker) meant there was little that could be offered to the child'. In certain cases, the willingness of other professionals to intercede with the families, such as the general
practitioner in the former case, and the 'huge support offered by
the school counsellor' in the latter case, made a considerable difference to the social workers' ability to intervene. The support of-

fered by social work managers, for example their willingness to do joint visits, also helped to temper relationships and was identified as another factor assisting social workers in building relationships with families. Equally, the opportunity for social workers to get support from their colleagues and managers enabled them to negotiate successfully when relationships were fragile.

Relationship with Other Professionals

Good relationships with other professionals and the availability of services from other professionals were identified by the social workers as significant factors affecting the ongoing management of child abuse cases. A worker commented:

> the co-operation of my colleagues has been great . . . the public health nurse has my phone number and will ring me when there is an emergency.

Links with social workers in other agencies were perceived as helpful, particularly when joint work and consultation was possible. Relationships were not always constructive however and in a few cases social workers identified problems in working with other professionals which constrained the management of their work. In one worker's view, lack of co-operation from the Gardaí made the work more difficult:

> . . . if the Gardaí had been more willing to address the child sexual abuse allegations with the father it would have helped the working relationship with him from my point of view . . . the father had been told that the Gardaí had been notified but they never went to see him to inform him or question him.

'Better working relations with psychology' would have made a difference in another case, and difficulty in arranging 'core group meetings' was detrimental to progress in another. The issue of inter-agency and inter-professional relationships is dealt with in more detail in Chapter Four, which reflects the views of all disciplines involved in child protection.

Pressure of Work and Support for Workers

In eight of the cases, social workers claimed that caseload size seriously limited the time they had available to give to active child abuse cases. The lack of time to work directly with children and 'not being able to offer support rather than just monitoring' were identified as particular negative effects on the intervention. All the workers were allocated cases on the basis of the 'patch'[6] system, rather than on their ability to take on extra work. Caseload 'weighting'[7] and changes in the 'overall management of cases' were suggested.

The lack of structural supports for workers, such as office accommodation, was also mentioned as a factor influencing case management. In one of the cases, the social worker described how the family lived twenty-four miles away from the nearest health centre. This severely restricted her ability to do individual work with the child:

> I should really be seeing the child out of home but there is
> no way I could take her all the way back to my office . . .
> there should be a local office.

Finally in at least one case, personal issues were identified by a worker as a possible factor affecting her management of a case. This worker had had a bereavement during a particularly difficult time in the case under discussion, and had therefore felt unable to offer sufficient support to the child. While she made the point that 'all the team were very supportive' she emphasised the impact of events like this on her ability to focus and make effective decisions.

It is clear from the accounts above that social workers had very clear ideas as to what factors enhance or limit their ability to operate. They highlight the importance of good support for workers, both in relation to supervision and practical structural supports. They also highlight again the crucial importance of good working relations with other professionals and with families in order to

---

[6] Social workers were attached to different geographical areas known as 'patches' and took on cases where the family address was in their area.

[7] 'Weighting' means measuring caseloads on the basis of the required input into each situation rather than simply their quantity.

achieve positive outcomes from their work. Many of the issues referred to above arise in later chapters relating to professionals and to parents, and will be explored further at that point.

C) Adequacy of Services Offered to Families

Another relevant issue regarding the ongoing management of the cases was considered to be the social workers' perception of the adequacy of the child protection service offered to clients. In addition to examining practice issues influencing progress in child abuse cases, we looked at the nature of services being offered to families, and the social workers' views on their adequacy or otherwise.

Under half of the social workers considered that clients were getting a satisfactory service from the Health Board. About a third felt this quite strongly, and in the other cases, social workers reported mixed views indicating that the child or children had received a good service but the parent(s) had not.

The services which were offered to families, and which the social workers considered useful, were defined in terms of service to the children, or services more broadly targeted at the families. They included the following:

- referral to other services, such as the Community Child Centre;

- good support and counselling for the child from a number of other professionals;

- support services such as the home maker;

- intensive social work support for the family;

- family therapy;

- group work for the child;

- care placement for the child.

Even though almost half of the respondents did regard the services to families as adequate, the majority of them could identify a number of additional services which were lacking, but which they considered important to improve the service offered. Crèche and day care facilities for children, and counselling and other services specifically for parents were particularly emphasised. It was also felt that families should have more social work intervention and that more therapeutic services should be available to families without the necessity to go on waiting lists for long periods. The lack of treatment services and the waiting list for the psychology service were also identified as key limitations in services to clients. In one case, the lack of foster placements was identified as a serious deficit in the service presently provided for the family in question. Social workers expressed the view that they should be working more therapeutically with families as a whole, particularly with the other children in the households, as opposed to just the victims of abuse and neglect.

Nearly all respondents identified the need for at least one other support service for the families they were working with. The most commonly cited were parenting groups for both mothers and fathers, and the availability of separate counselling for parents. Similarly, the lack of youth activities, after school groups and adolescent groups were identified by many as limitations in services given to families. More practical services, outside of Health Board control, such as accommodation and improved public transport which would enable clients to attend services were also recommended.

CONCLUSION

Interviews with social workers in relation to the initial and ongoing stages of intervention with the sample cases produced a number of significant findings. In summary these relate to: the centrality of social workers in the child protection system; social workers' views on and implementation of procedures and guidelines; social workers' views on progress in the cases they worked with; the factors affecting social workers' ongoing management of cases; and social workers' views on the adequacy of services offered by the SEHB social worker service to their clients.

Centrality of Social Workers in the Child Protection System

One consistent finding in relation to both the initial stage of intervention and the ongoing management of cases was the centrality of social workers in the process, even where they themselves were not having direct ongoing involvement with the families in question. Despite the fact that social workers themselves are unlikely to be the referrers of alleged child abuse and neglect, they were almost always the profession who notified the alleged abuse to the DCC. We also found that the notification meetings were most likely to: a) endorse the recommendations made by social workers in their preliminary reports to the meetings; and b) to advise certain action to be taken by the social worker as a first step in responding to the allegations. Where other professional or agency involvement was recommended, this was almost always in addition to, as opposed to instead of, social work involvement.

Procedures and Guidelines

Social workers generally recognised the importance of procedures such as child abuse notification meetings and child care planning meetings. However, a certain level of scepticism was reflected by the interviewees in relation to the relevance of such procedures, and some suggestions were put forward as to how they could be made more meaningful. For example, a number of social workers suggested the notification meetings procedure would be enhanced if social workers themselves were to attend to represent certain complex issues. The fact that formal child care plans were not used in any of the cases raises questions as to their usefulness and relevance for social workers in everyday practice. Workers who were operating alone in cases, for example, did not see the point of written plans, whereas some value was ascribed to such an approach where a number of other personnel were involved in the cases. On the other hand, in the absence of a formal system of planning, it was found that reviews and updates of plans for children and families seemed to be left primarily to the discretion of the individual social workers.

Progress in Interventions with Families

Progress appeared to be a difficult concept to measure, and in general, social workers' views on the outcomes to date in their cases were quite mixed. While child protection concerns were considered to have been addressed satisfactorily in some cases, problems in the broader family context were most often considered to be ongoing and often unchanging. Two important points emanate from this finding. Firstly, it illuminates the way in which the social work system tended to focus almost exclusively and narrowly on issues relating directly to the child abuse and neglect issues, and, secondly, it shows the way in which social workers themselves tended to define progress primarily in similarly narrow terms. This finding reflects a trend in social work with children and families internationally; systems have shifted more and more towards a risk oriented approach to child care issues, and away from a broader child welfare discourse (Parton, 1991, 1996). Despite the rhetoric of promoting welfare within the Irish *Child Care Act, 1991*, services for children and families have been progressively ghettoised into the limited sphere of child 'abuse' and child 'neglect'. The reasons and rationale for this are complex and will be discussed in more detail in the final chapter when the full ambit of the research has been documented.

Factors Affecting Social Workers' Ongoing Management of Child Abuse and Neglect Cases

Findings from this aspect of the research highlight the many factors which influence a social worker's ability to carry out their social work mandate successfully. Personal and professional support by way of supervision was identified most often as the key determining factor affecting social workers' management of cases. While formal supervision was found to be, on the whole, inadequate, the majority of social workers expressed satisfaction with the level of informal support they received from managers. However, given the complexity of the work being undertaken, the need for more formal support and an opportunity to reflect on one's work was identified as a crucial factor in assisting social workers to carry out their work successfully. In addition to supervision, more practical structural elements appeared to influence significantly the social workers' own progress in their work. Basic amenities such as office space, adequate security in health centres and access to telephones were lacking in many instances and were found to have a direct negative effect on the work being carried out. Support and good working relationships with other professionals also determined how well social workers felt they could do their jobs. Each of these issues is discussed in more detail later in the book but the frequency with which social workers referred to these factors emphasises the fact that practitioners, despite their central role in the child protection process, cannot operate in isolation from their managers and professional colleagues, nor can they adequately deliver services without the most basic of structural supports.

Adequacy of Services Offered

Social workers realistically identified the limitations in the service they were offering to families. Even where workers considered their clients to have received an adequate service, they all recognised significant areas for improvement. This was most frequently framed in terms of a need for more support services and a need for social workers to have smaller caseloads in order to have sufficient time to devote to the families they were working with. Reflected in the interviewees' responses was a desire to provide more than the minimum 'child protection' service in the form of more preventative and therapeutic services to families.

As many of the issues raised by social workers in this chapter emerge throughout our analysis of interviews with clients and with other professionals, it seems premature to make general postulations and conclusions. The following three chapters will illuminate further the key issues relating to both the initial investigation and ongoing management of cases of child abuse and neglect.

CHAPTER FOUR

PROFESSIONAL ROLES, RESPONSIBILITIES AND INTER-AGENCY CO-OPERATION

INTRODUCTION

Under the *Child Abuse Guidelines* (Department of Health, 1987), social workers have been allocated the 'key' role in child abuse and neglect cases. However, the document also underlines the importance of the 'ready willingness and co-operation of the staffs of hospitals, GPs, Garda Síochána, schools and many non-statutory agencies' (p. 9). Examining only the contribution of the social workers in the region would therefore exclude the very important role played by other professionals, and for that reason the study focused on a wide range of practitioners.

In reality, the child protection network contains many members whose primary vocational role may not necessarily be geared solely to the task of protecting children, but whose involvement with children and families is crucial to the overall task of maintaining their safety and welfare. For most of the practitioners who featured in this research, child protection was an important, but not central, element of their professional practice. However in many instances their involvement was close and even sometimes on a daily basis, and could be considered essential in the ongoing management of cases.

As the findings from the first part of the study have shown, a number of practitioners were, or had until recently, been involved in various ways with the eighteen cases which formed our sample. These comprised school teachers, a school counsellor, a homemaker, Gardaí, child care workers both in Community Care and from residential settings, a psychologist, social workers from services and agencies other than Community Care, and public health nurses. In all, we carried out twenty interviews with these professionals, and formed a picture of an active inter-professional network. The findings will be considered in this chapter under the following headings: child protection roles and responsibilities; frequency of contact with families; nature of professional involvement; and impact of inter-disciplinary interventions. The next chapter will deal with the issue of working relationships between different disciplines.

PROFESSIONAL INVOLVEMENT IN CHILD PROTECTION WORK

When asked about their involvement in the child protection process, the majority of practitioners in the child protection network identified 'referral' and 'notification' of abuse as their principal obligations. Teachers added 'monitoring' to this, and the school counsellor saw her job as being 'to support students who have made disclosures and need help'. Those employed in specialist treatment areas recognised their therapeutic function, and the public health nurses, child care workers and home help saw themselves as having important ongoing therapeutic and monitoring functions with families after the abuse had been diagnosed. It was very clear that none of these professionals, apart from the Gardaí, saw themselves as having any role in the *investigation* of child abuse or responsibility for preventing its re-occurrence, though the non Community Care social workers (those working in child psychiatry or voluntary agencies) felt that 'in practice' this function was occasionally thrust upon them. For example, a local authority social worker who, as he described it, did not have an 'official monitoring role' would, particularly with travellers, 'do monitoring for the Health Boards where there are concerns but where these are not sufficient for the Health Boards to be brought in'.

In general, most professionals whom we interviewed expressed satisfaction with their child protection roles, but on occasion felt that their positions were misunderstood, undervalued or that there were unrealistic expectations of what they could do. A social worker employed in the child psychiatric service said that she is 'often expected to take on child protection concerns . . . address allegations' and 'can often get hassle about not doing the child protection work' from the Community Care team. A school principal felt that sometimes 'school is being used for community based problems'. A public health nurse felt that the important role that her profession plays should be recognised more by senior management 'in terms of support, in-service training, competence to fill out forms, report writing, attendance at case conferences'. A residential worker felt that the role of her hostel was misunderstood:

> . . . there seems to be a difference of opinion . . . different expectations from managers down to social workers, due to a lack of places elsewhere . . . the child care worker is not given enough status . . . they are often treated as glorified baby-sitting.

Another residential child care worker, while satisfied with her role, felt its importance was not appreciated:

> . . . it needs to be more recognised . . . we are front line people, we deal with the children on a day-to-day basis . . .

A psychologist expressed frustration that other professionals had initially expected her simply to do cognitive testing, and tended not to acknowledge the full range of her skills, including therapeutic work.

Two other practitioners, a home help and a family therapist, included 'seeing that children are protected' as part of their function. Despite the very active and important contributions these professionals were making to the protection and welfare of the children they were involved with, the main responsibility for child protection was seen to be the domain of the Community Care social worker. A child care worker, describing her job, said: 'I like it . . . I have no responsibility at the end of the day . . . the social worker has that . . .' In another case, where the parents refused to co-operate with the Health Boards, a school counsellor had taken over, but not willingly: 'I feel the school has been left holding the baby . . . I don't object to this but it is the Health Board's responsibility'.

Ultimately, some practitioners felt that being identified with the child protection role might hinder their relationships with families, as expressed by one public health nurse:

I thought she might see it as an 'us and them situation', and
I didn't want to be on 'them' side. I felt if I didn't remain
friendly with her, she wasn't going to let anyone else in.

FREQUENCY OF CONTACT WITH FAMILIES

The majority of the non-social work professionals whom we interviewed had ongoing contact with the children and families,
ranging in frequency from once to five times per week. These were
the teachers, the home help, the Community Care child care
worker, one residential worker, and public health nurses. The
family therapist and the psychologist whom we interviewed saw
the families or children on a regular weekly or fortnightly basis.

Of the other professionals, a community psychiatric nurse
would have seen the mother of the children concerned approximately once a month. Another residential child care worker, who
had previous involvement, and a school counsellor were in touch
on an occasional basis, mainly with the children, 'if there are any
problems' or 'when she gets upset'. The non-Community Care social workers had relatively infrequent contact, which would normally be in response to a particular incident or request from the
families. Contact between the Gardaí and the families was similarly sporadic, mainly centring around occasions when there was
a development in a prosecution for child sexual abuse, and in two
of the four cases where we interviewed gardaí, there was no contact between them and the families at all.

NATURE OF PROFESSIONAL INVOLVEMENT

As indicated earlier in Phase One, professional involvement
tended to relate to specific areas of work. Two of the practitioners
we interviewed, a teacher and a public health nurse, no longer
had any contact with the particular cases because either they or
the children had moved elsewhere, but their replacements had
continued the work on the same basis and with the same frequency.

Teachers had ongoing and important supportive roles to play
in monitoring and supporting the children who were at school. In
at least one case the teacher felt that the child concerned 'has to

be watched constantly . . . to protect other children from her and her from others', and, in another, the teacher had to mediate between rival factions of the child's family. A school counsellor was working with a child whose family deliberately broke off contact with the Health Board, to provide support to her while in school 'when she is upset or wants to talk'. Public health nurses were carrying out routine work acting in their normal roles with families who have young children, but with more intensive visiting.

The Community Care child care worker and the home maker were doing 'parenting' work as well as direct work with the children themselves. Two children, in different cases, had been in care for short periods and in each situation, a key residential child care worker had stayed in touch with the family. One was doing ongoing work with a child and her parent 'to settle her back home' and the involvement of the other residential worker was more in response to contacts from the child herself. The community psychiatric nurse was an important support person for a mother in one case, and provided her with a link to the psychiatric services.

Social workers from the County Council were involved in relation to housing issues for two particular families, and most of their contact was in relation to this. The principal involvement of the other practitioners who included a psychiatric social worker, a family therapist and a psychologist concerned either ongoing therapy with families or, in one case, with an individual child.

Almost all the practitioners reported good working relationships with the children and families, though their contact with parents tended to be with mothers rather than fathers who, when they were present[1] appeared more difficult to engage. The one exception to this good working relationship was where mistrust had developed between the family concerned and the County Council.

IMPACT OF INTERDISCIPLINARY INTERVENTIONS ON THE SAMPLE CASES

The majority of practitioners were able to identify positive aspects of their interventions, and, in the main, they were satisfied that

---

[1] As indicated earlier, a number of the parents in the study were lone female carers.

they had made some contribution to enhancing the protection and welfare of the children they were involved with. Like the social workers, they were able to report progress in some areas but not in others. Where some form of therapy was being provided, it appeared to work well. For example a psychologist who worked with a sexual abuse victim gave positive feedback:

> . . . it may take years for the child to address the various problems for her in therapy but I feel that a trusting relationship has been built up and child opens up more and more to me.

Likewise, a child guidance social worker was pleased with the insights gained by children she was working with:

> The girls have improved in that they used to always play their parents off against one another but now do so less . . . they appear to have more insight into the family situation and the family circumstances . . . and into the issues around the separation . . . more aware that they are not the only ones who are in this situation.

Family support work appeared to be effective where it was being carried out. For example, a home maker who engaged to work with a mother and her children, who had been physically and sexually abused by her former partner, was happy with the changes she observed:

> Big progress. The little boy has become very outgoing, he has no fears out there, not like before. There has been a big change in the older children, they are not fearful and they were very scared before when the boyfriend was there.

Child care workers were also able to see the benefit of their input:

> Absolutely . . . the relationship between mother and child has improved . . . at first there was no contact at all from the family . . . they blamed [child] for the break-up of the family and for making the disclosure . . . she was blamed for bringing Gardaí and social services into their family . . . she was very confused and unhappy . . . used placement as time to get herself together . . . dealt with a number of issues . . .

there has been progress through the various meetings with the mother . . . move home has been successful . . .

There were a few situations were progress seemed limited to particular aspects of the children's and families' lives. One example was given by a school counsellor:

There has only been progress in so far as in the school . . . if there had not been a guidance counsellor in the school I really do not know what this girl would have done . . . by the time the social worker got involved she was so distrustful and let down by the Health Boards that there would have been no progress . . . so she was lucky as there are not counsellors in every school . . . but the parents are refusing to have any contact, they do not know of her problems and issues and this is very difficult for her . . .

Poor parental co-operation could be problematic at times. A family therapist reported how 'the parents are using the children between them . . . it's very hard to know, or to measure progress'. The unavailability or restricted nature of certain services appeared to impede progress in certain cases. A child care worker was quite concerned about one of her families:

The one- and two-year-old badly need to be assessed, so does the bigger lad. The psychologists won't see more than one child from the children's home . . . there should be flexibility around that . . . I'm not happy about it . . . the psychologists make their own rules . . . the staff in the children's home need a plan, they need to be able to sit down and talk to the child and he needs to be assessed first.

In some instances, the limitations were very obvious, despite the level of attention a case was receiving. It was recognised that the balance between 'good enough parenting' and less than adequate care was a difficult one to judge. A teacher expressed her frustration about the quality of life of a little girl in her class, but felt the father was difficult to work with and the Health Board were doing their best:

Well . . . the child has started school and is now starting day foster care so that's progress. She is very moody and atten-

tion seeking in school . . . but she isn't getting proper parenting . . . she has a very lurid imagination and is like a
child that watches too much TV and is up too late at night.
She lacks a stable environment . . . the father is very awk-
ward. I find him difficult to talk to . . . I can't relate to people not like myself . . . I'm afraid of him, would be very
wary.

Delays in the legal system appeared detrimental to progress in
other cases, some families 'waiting so long for the prosecution'
that they are under continuous strain. The difficulty in even
achieving prosecutions caused frustration, and, according to a
Garda sergeant, 'the DPP [Director of Public Prosecutions] is becoming judge and jury instead of letting a judge and jury decide
the outcome of a case'. These findings again highlight the uncertain nature of child protection work, illustrating how outcomes
can be influenced by many extraneous factors, even when the co-
operation and service of other agencies is engaged.

In summary, we found that in the majority of cases which we
examined, important and effective work was being carried out
with families and children by a combination of professionals,
many of whom were outside the statutory services, but were still
significant members of the child protection network. While most
professionals outside of the Community Care social work teams
had a limited view of their child protection role, they took this aspect of their work seriously and valued the acknowledgement they
got for it. Most of these practitioners had frequent contact with
the families involved. Interventions were judged to be successful
in the main, but like the social workers, practitioners in the wider
child protection network reported different levels of progress, and
felt occasionally hindered by other factors, such non co-operation
of parents and deficits in services. They acknowledged that their
own inputs were limited to particular aspects of the cases.

It is important to note that in five of the cases in our sample,
Health Boards social workers had little or no contact with the
families. In two cases, families were adamant that they wanted no
contact with the Health Boards, and in three others, the social
workers were new and somehow had not engaged with the families to the same extent as their predecessors, particularly as the

urgency of the initial referral had, at this stage, dissipated to some degree and the 'risk' was deemed to be contained. The input of non social work professionals was of particular importance in at least three of these cases, even though they did not perceive themselves to have, or in some cases want, overall responsibility for monitoring. This was despite the reality that there was no other input apart from theirs. The evidence reflected in this study that the 'policing' element of child protection work does not appeal to non-social work professional concurs with findings elsewhere. Butler (1996), in an exploration of the role of public health nurses in the Irish child protection system, suggests that the reluctance of non social work professionals to take on this mantle emanates from 'clashes of professional culture' (p. 310) which themselves can be traced to the ambivalence which exists in Ireland about state intrusion into the family. As a consequence, he points out, social workers are 'burdened with the "unenviable task" of carrying out the social control functions of child protection activity'. While the child abuse guidelines undoubtedly allocate central responsibility to social workers, it is obvious from what we found that a great deal of co-ordinated activity necessarily goes into child protection work. This is an aspect which requires addressing, both in terms of acknowledging the important contributions of those who are carrying out the most essential tasks, but also in the recognition that, while the health boards must retain overall responsibility, each practitioner must be accountable for the part he or she plays.

INTER-AGENCY CO-OPERATION

Inter-disciplinary and inter-agency work is generally regarded as central to good child protection practice. The *Department of Health Child Abuse Guidelines* (Department of Health, 1987) have identified it as an 'essential and integral element of the professional task of attempting to protect children from abuse' (p. 9). Child abuse inquiries have also emphasised the necessity to pay attention to the need to provide families and children with a co-ordinated service. Given the complexity involved in identifying child abuse, particularly by professionals whose primary vocational role is not in that area, and given the diverse backgrounds of the various members of the child protection network, inter-agency co-operation is generally regarded in the literature as fraught with difficulties. Studies by Hallett and Stevenson (1980), Reder, Duncan and Gray (1993) and Hallett and Birchall (1992) have highlighted some of the problems in working together in child protection, and child abuse inquiries have repeatedly pointed to the serious consequences of its failure. The literature suggests that problems of role confusion, absence of shared understanding, different ethical norms and vocational orientations as well as professional rivalries, assumptions about status and stereotyping all contribute to inter-agency and inter-professional tensions in child protection work. Bearing this in mind, we set out to explore the working relationships in the sample cases. Generally, it must be said, we found a willingness to co-operate with each other and a recognition of the necessity for doing so, some workers identifying 'awareness and respect for each other's roles' and a 'willingness to meet and make contact' as positive factors. The value of joint assessment was acknowledged, and the importance of mutual support was emphasised.

Positive aspects of inter-agency and inter-professional work were identified by all the practitioners who were interviewed, particularly with regard to the pooling of skills and resources, the way in which different practitioners facilitated each other's work. They also commented on the effectiveness of their contact and communication, the support and mutual respect they offered each other, and the type of personal or informal relationships that existed between them. These elements of positive co-ordination will now be examined separately.

Pooling of Skills and Resources

The value of joint work, including joint assessment, and pooling of expertise were clearly appreciated. Practitioners in general had a regard and respect for the particular 'wisdom' held by each individual profession; for example, a teacher was very positive, firstly, about the extent to which the public health nurse and the social worker were knowledgeable about the children concerned, and secondly, that they were prepared to share that knowledge with her. The 'brokering' skills of a social worker who mediated between the housing authorities and a family were praised. The 'outside perspective' of a family therapist who worked closely with the Health Boards was greatly valued. The sharing of practical tasks between a medical social worker and the Community Care team made for a more efficient service delivery, and the fact that a home maker 'had child protection as a priority' ensured a co-ordinated approach in a particular case. Teachers seemed to be willing to make contributions beyond the teaching role, such as contacting previous schools to help build up a picture of the child's history, and enabling a child who had returned from care to settle back into the school with minimal disruption.

Facilitation of Each Other's Work

Many examples were given of the willingness of professionals to work together and facilitate each other. The flexibility shown by schools who allowed other workers to interview children on the premises was clearly valuable. The willingness of teachers and a school counsellor to give particular children ongoing support and attention and to continue their involvement at all levels was highlighted. The Community Child Centre was seen as 'flexible and obliging', and the Gardaí in particular acknowledged the willingness of the unit to facilitate joint interviewing. Equally, child care workers were seen as helpful in organising reviews, and enabling social workers and children to meet on the premises.

Good Contact and Communication

One of the child protection practices most highly valued was the responsiveness of professionals when their involvement was re-quested. Teachers in particular acknowledged a need for 'outside contact' when they were experiencing difficulties or concerns about particular children. Those whom we interviewed had experienced prompt responses from social workers and public health nurses to their requests for a visit to the school. To quote a teacher: 'The fact that the last time I asked for help the social worker came out, she sat and listened . . . the public health nurse knows everything . . . they are really on the ball.'

Regular communication appeared to exist between Health Board and non-Health Board social workers, and shared information and regular meetings between a psychologist and social worker in one case seemed helpful. Contact between social workers and public health nurses was good in the majority of cases, and the location of community psychiatric nurses in health centres helped to establish regular exchange of information. Professionals outside the Board, such as the family therapist, and residential child care workers, also reported that they had regular and useful meetings with psychologists, and social workers.

Support

Mutual support in difficult child protection work was identified as essential to all practitioners. While supervision was seen as the responsibility of line managers, the type of informal support offered by 'peers' was highly rated. A home maker described how drained she became at times:

> I still get emotional when I think about it . . . what happened to those children . . . but I can go and talk to the social worker or the nurse and talk to them about it. I am very close to the situation . . . I get emotionally involved with the children.

A public health nurse working in an area which was known to be difficult appreciated the extra contact and affirmation she received from the senior social worker. A Community Care child care worker found the 'team atmosphere' very positive in the health centre where she was based.

Mutual Respect and Value for Each Other's Roles

'Solidarity', between a social worker and a psychologist, in one case, and general respect for each other's roles, seemed to enhance the quality of their work, and also acted as a guard against isolation. The sense that her contributions were valued was important to a public health nurse, and child care workers appreciated being treated as 'equals' by social workers and teachers. The 'general awareness and respect for each other's roles' shared between social workers from the Health Boards and the County Council appeared to be good for their working relationships.

Personal Relationships

The most frequently mentioned inter-agency and inter-professional issue was the importance of personal relationships between workers. The fact of working in the same health centre, and the fact that some workers had been in the one post for a number of years contributed to this. Face-to-face contact, and acquaintance with the particular professional was rated very highly by teachers. Gardaí prioritised 'the opportunity to meet' as the most important aspect of inter-professional relations; '. . . knowing the individual social worker makes it much easier'.

The social aspects of team work, for example having lunch together, or going out at night, were judged by a child care worker to enhance trust and co-operation. A public health nurse greatly valued the social worker's habit of 'dropping in for a cup of coffee' where they would discuss cases and 'bounce things around a bit' using the opportunity to re-assess their intervention. Informal contact between Health Board social workers and those in the County Council and child guidance services also helped them to maintain a co-ordinated approach to their clients.

We asked practitioners to identify any problems they had working together in child protection. Some of these perceived differences concerned issues over which no agency had complete control. Others concerned inter-personal or professional matters, which could potentially be improved by fostering mutual understanding, and improving work practices generally. The difficulties which we did encounter can be categorised into three areas: structural/organisational factors which impacted on inter-agency co-operation; problems with feedback and communication; and disagreement over professional roles and responsibilities.

Structural Factors which Impacted on Inter-agency Co-operation

Delays of one sort or another caused frustration to practitioners, interfering with their ability to co-ordinate their own work with that of other disciplines and agencies. For example, having to wait several weeks for an appointment at the child sexual abuse assessment service meant that the Gardaí had to postpone the collection of vital evidence. Frustration with the waiting list for the psychology service provoked some workers to suggest that this area needed some re-prioritising so that urgent cases were seen quickly.

The slowness of the legal system was identified as a source of occasional tension between the Gardaí and the Health Board workers, and likewise, the Gardaí lamented the lack of a 'call out' system for social workers at weekends.[2] Sometimes, families had moved either from other Health Boards regions, or other jurisdictions, and there were some complaints about the tardy transfer of information between these areas.

Some of the professionals we saw had particularly busy schedules, which did not always allow them time to fit in child protection work; for example the normal teaching day did not really accommodate meetings for teachers. Teachers protested that they could not give sufficient time and attention to visiting professionals and felt that they missed potentially worthwhile opportunities to share information.

Although none of the above was judged to be particularly dangerous in terms of increasing the risk of child abuse, practitioners acknowledged that they caused delays in decision making, and made their work with families more difficult than it needed to be.

Problems with Feedback and Communication

One of the factors which impeded good communication appeared to be the perennial problem of staff changes, particularly among social workers. This caused some frustration to other professionals, particularly those who would not necessarily have frequent contact with them. Teachers, Gardaí, public health nurses and social workers outside the Health Board expressed the wish to be kept informed of staff changes within their areas, not to wait until there was a problem to get in touch. For example a local authority social worker commented:

> When social workers are leaving and new ones coming, an effort should be made to introduce them to various professionals and agencies involved . . . It's very unhelpful to ring

[2] Working relationships between the Gardaí and other child protection workers will be dealt with in a separate section

up looking for a worker and find that they have left and
have been replaced.

Another common problem identified by schools in particular was
the lack of 'feedback particularly after a case conference'. Some
teachers complained that they rarely heard back from psychologists who had assessed children in their classes, having requested
information from the school: '. . . to mention psychologists to
teachers is like putting a red rag to a bull . . . they send out pages
of notes to fill in and send us back nothing.'

In another case, a teacher commented on the absence of contact
from a social worker over several months:

> I am sort of a link between [the child] and the social serv-
> ices . . . because of the parents' non co-operation I have had
> a lot of contact with the social worker . . . yet she hasn't
> phoned me since January and I don't know why . . .

Generally, the need for more links between various professionals
and agencies was proposed, including a 'forum for statutory and
voluntary agencies to come together', more regular meetings
'outside of child abuse concerns' and a desire to establish better
links between Gardaí, social workers, and schools.

All members of the professional network recognised the need for
confidential treatment of information, but in some cases, resented
the fact that they were not trusted, or privy to certain aspects of
decision making and found this detrimental to working together. A
child care worker, for example, found the psychologist's reluctance
to share information on a mutual client quite unhelpful to her own
work, and a public health nurse, who felt she was excluded from
decision making, said: 'it's a problem when you don't know what's
going on . . . confidentiality is important . . . but . . .'

Professional Roles and Responsibilities

The study indicated that most professionals were clear about
their roles in relation to child protection duties and responsibilities. However, there was a minority of instances where assumptions appeared to exist which had not necessarily been agreed be-
forehand. There was an apparent expectation that social workers

outside of Community Care, for example, in the County Council, or in the child psychiatric service, would 'take on a child protection role'. Where this was agreed and had definite limitations, it appeared to work very well. Where it was not agreed, it became a source of tension. A child guidance social worker commented:

> There can often be difficulty working with the Community Care social workers . . . a lack of clarity about roles . . . we are often expected to take on child protection concerns and allegations . . . often get hassle about not doing the child protection work from the rest of the Community Care team . . . there is an unwillingness to accept the particular role of the child guidance social worker . . . there can be an expectation that I should be doing similar work and have similar responsibility.

In some cases, social workers felt that other members of the child protection network could have taken a bigger share of the burden of responsibility. In one instance, a social worker cited an example of how a referral had been passed through two other professionals (a public health nurse and a general practitioner) before it reached her. Neither of these practitioners had seen it as their responsibility to formally notify the case, despite the fact that they had had more first hand contact with the situation. While the social workers we interviewed considered their colleagues in other disciplines to be supportive, they felt that their involvement was quite limited. 'Although others are prepared to do their bit, everyone sees it as the social worker's responsibility'. Social workers claimed that having to take full responsibility prevented them from prioritising their work. Unlike some of their colleagues, they lacked 'autonomy in deciding what bits to do'. According to one social worker, there was a particular difficulty with the psychology service:

> . . . the psychology department was dismissive of this case . . . did their bit and then closed it . . . their impression was that the social worker had the full responsibility for the case, they just took on one bit of it . . . I feel this is a general problem with psychology . . . they also make an assumption that social workers do all of the 'go for' work, even in cases they are not actively involved [in] . . . certain psychologists

expect the social worker to do the running around and collecting.

But, paradoxically, the study also highlighted a need for recognition that some practitioners had roles which were neither statutory, nor directly related to investigation of child abuse, but were equally important in the longer term management of cases. The fact that 'social workers are the ones who have all of the power' was considered by a child care worker to undermine her own profession's valuable role in longer term monitoring and assessment. Other practitioners perceived themselves to be undervalued or misunderstood in various ways. A public health nurse suggested that her professional colleagues 'have a perception that their information is not as valuable as the next professional', and 'lack of self-esteem' about teachers' abilities in relation to child protection work was perceived by a member of that discipline as an impediment to team functioning.

Sometimes it appeared that acknowledgement of the value of a particular contribution was lacking in practical terms. For example, a family therapist providing an obviously valuable service to the Health Board was not currently being reimbursed. The need for better understanding by management of the role and function of residential units in terms of funding was highlighted by one child care worker.

The impact of these factors on inter-agency and inter-professional co-ordination needs to be judged in the context of the many positive examples of joint work which were highlighted in the research. Suggestions to further improve relationships and overcome some of the difficulties just outlined included the need to establish a protocol for an organised, planned approach to families, which would prevent important issues 'falling between two stools', and also avoid any overlap of visiting. The need to address any divisions and difficulties between professionals, and also to introduce a level of flexibility, avoiding over-rigid demarcation of roles were proposed. However, the most significant and often repeated suggestions concerned the desirability of more informal and formal meetings between professionals. It was acknowledged that increasing the number of meetings would put further pressure on existing workloads, but it was suggested that

these gatherings could be aimed at discussing child welfare concerns in a seminar type forum, or as training days for various aspects of child protection work. It was considered that a useful by-
product of such meetings would be an increase in personal contact
and opportunities to meet one another informally.

We decided to separate our findings concerning Garda/Health
Board relations from the other aspects of inter-agency and inter-
professional work, because of the recent introduction of guidelines
for the *Notification of Suspected Cases of Child Abuse Between the
Health Boards and the Gardaí*. The issues which were highlighted
are described below under the headings of: differing approaches of
Gardaí and other child protection professionals; feedback and
continuity of involvement; communication and exchange of information between the Health Boards and the Gardaí; specialisation;
and, finally, training.

WORKING WITH THE GARDAÍ

In April 1995, the Department of Health introduced guidelines for
*Notification of Suspected Cases of Child Abuse between the Health
Boards and the Gardaí*. Previous research in Ireland (Buckley,
1992, 1995) indicated that, despite willingness on the parts of
both Gardaí and Health Board child protection workers to co-
operate, certain difficulties existed, such as differing professional
objectives, lack of agreement over confidentiality, and difficulty in
exchange of information due to varying work patterns. The guidelines had only been in operation for a matter of months when this
study was conducted, so the impact of their implementation had
scarcely been experienced.

All the professionals whom we interviewed were positive about
the introduction of the Gardaí/Health Boards notification guidelines, seeing them as 'helpful in clarifying each other's role', preventing 'informal and unreliable contact', and promoting more
contact between the Health Board and the Gardaí. It was suggested that guidelines provide 'protection, cover and clarity' and
provide a 'framework for guiding practice'.

Some reservations were declared, however, about the 'black and
white' nature of the procedures, which did not allow for the 'grey
areas in complex child abuse cases'. A certain amount of ambiva-

lence was expressed over the need to refer *all* cases of abuse and neglect, even when concerns were vague and unclear. The usefulness of referring certain situations, for example, the case of an elderly man who was caught 'flashing', was queried, and it was felt that informal discussions and formal notification were confused at times. However, in general, agreement existed about the usefulness and necessity of the guidelines, which most practitioners agreed had improved working relationships, and affirmed the role of the Gardaí in child protection.

Social workers reported that they were now experiencing better co-ordination with the Gardaí than they had in previous years. Other professionals, including child care workers and teachers, gave examples of co-operation with the Gardaí in dealing with particular problems, such as children 'running away' and poor school attendance. There were also reports of 'good communication and sharing of information' between Gardaí and professionals, and the Gardaí themselves felt that there was a much better mutual understanding between the professions. However, despite such reported improvements in the working relationships between the Gardaí and child protection workers, some difficulties emerged in this study which seemed to be detrimental to joint work and ultimately to the children and families involved. These concerned: the differences in approach between gardaí and other workers; problems with feedback; inability to communicate with particular Gardaí; difficulties in accessing information; and reliance on 'personalities'.

Differing Approaches of Gardaí and Other Child Protection Professions

It was generally accepted that the principal functions of Gardaí and child protection workers are different, the main goal of the Gardaí being to detect crime and ultimately bring about a successful prosecution, and the goals of other workers being generally more welfare orientated. Related to this, strong views were expressed by the various practitioners that, despite the greater emphasis on child protection, Gardaí still lack a 'basic understanding' of the complexities of many of the clients' social and family situations, '[they] can be unsympathetic with homeless families', can look at things in a 'cut and dried way' and can be 'judgmental'. It was suggested that the 'variance' of Gardaí was problematic; 'some are in tune with client groups, other times the approaches clash because of the barefaced authority that the Gardaí use'. Many practitioners commented that the attitudes and personalities of individual gardaí really determined the quality of co-operative working, and that 'knowing' the particular officer was crucial.

There appeared to be some conflict with regard to the issue of confidentiality between the Gardaí and others. While several non-Garda professionals felt the Gardaí were 'not appreciative of confidentiality', one garda was critical of the way that social workers would, unwisely in his view, very quickly 'reveal their sources' when investigating referrals.

Feedback and Continuity of Involvement

Although it was accepted that legal matters, such as the decision to mount a prosecution, were beyond the control of the Gardaí, practitioners from different disciplines were critical of the Gardaí's failure to pursue certain investigations, and felt that the low prosecution rate for sex offenders in particular could be improved. 'Gardaí not getting back to you' was identified as a problem, and there were complaints that 'you never hear . . . unless you keep following them up'. While it was also recognised that the perceived slowness in gathering evidence was not always in the Gardaí's control, practitioners were very critical of the delay in getting cases to court 'given how traumatic involvement with the Gardaí usually is for clients'.

Feasibility of Communicating with Gardaí and Accessing Information

Replicating previous research on this subject (Buckley, 1993, 1995), this study also found a lot of evidence indicating difficulties on the part of social workers in contacting particular gardaí and in accessing information in their absence. Despite previous assurances that one designated officer would have overall responsibility for particular cases (Department of Health, 1995), the social workers found this not to be the case. One worker commented that 'the problem is getting a different garda each time . . . they don't have a particular garda assigned, though they said they would'.

Even where one specific officer is involved in a case, social workers found that 'there can be a delay of two to three weeks in making a contact' due to shift changes. They also found that no records of the case existed in the station; Gardaí, other than the officer involved, were unable to provide any information of the case.

Need for Specialisation

There was strong support for the appointment of specialist or designated Garda officers in child protection, which, it was felt, would address many of the difficulties outlined above. It was generally considered that trust and knowledge could be built up between specialist Gardaí and other child protection practitioners, overcoming communication problems and allowing for more efficient and less traumatic investigation of allegations. This suggestion was also supported by the gardaí whom we interviewed, who felt the appointment of specialist child protection Gardaí would be 'an ideal situation'.

Training

Recent training initiatives had been very positively received, and all professionals were keen to have this on an ongoing basis. It was also proposed that training should be extended to all members of the Gardaí, not just senior officers.

Other suggestions for improvements in working relationships and better Gardaí/child protection worker practice included the setting up of meetings and local committees to keep lines of communication open and to develop links.

CONCLUSION

In summary, this research has shown that interventions into the cases were carried out by a number of different professionals, both inside and outside the Health Board. The value of co-ordinated work and pooling of resources was appreciated by everyone involved, and there was evidence of good co-operation. Where inter-agency and inter-professional difficulties existed, they were primarily related to structural factors, such as delays and waiting lists for services, and to problems with feedback and communication. Failure to share information in some instances caused irritation, and misunderstandings about roles and responsibilities sometimes occurred. Community Care social workers felt somewhat over-burdened with responsibility for child protection, while some of their colleagues had more freedom to prioritise and manage their work. On the other hand, the importance of the roles played by other professionals was unacknowledged in some instances.

Despite recent training initiatives and more attention to co-operative working, some difficulties still impacted on Health Board/Gardaí relationships. The differing orientations of both professions sometimes caused tensions, and there were disagreements over the best ways to approach families, and issues of confidentiality. Problems of feedback and communication still existed; the 'unavailability' of gardaí and the lack of specialist posts were identified as impediments to efficient working.

These inter-agency and inter-professional difficulties need to be seen in the context of much good co-operative practice which was happening in the region at the time of the study. The benefits gained from the pooling of resources, offering of mutual support and practical help, and respect for each other's contributions were very evident. The value and importance of personal relationships and informal contact was emphasised, an aspect of inter-agency and inter-professional co-operation which also featured strongly in a recent British study (Hallett, 1995). However, as Hallett suggests, caution must be exercised in relation to reliance on informal relationships which depend on 'personalities'. While it is good to see that the interest and commitment of individuals does impact on the work, relationships can be disrupted when people move jobs, and the system should not rely on or assume the willingness or capacity of staff to get on well together. Attention must also be paid to the facilitation of co-ordinated work in a formal sense, as well as facilitating friendly relationships.

The role played by case conferences in the child protection system is crucial in terms of co-ordinating investigation and assessment, and also provides an important forum to facilitate good working relationships between different child protection professionals. The next chapter looks in detail at this aspect of child protection 'machinery'.

CHAPTER FIVE

CASE CONFERENCES

INTRODUCTION

Case conferences have been allocated a central position in the *Department of Health Child Abuse Guidelines* (1987) as 'an essential feature of inter-agency co-operation' (p. 18), and their importance has been emphasised in both the guidelines for *Notification of Cases of Suspected Child Abuse between Health Boards and the Gardaí* and the *Report of the Kilkenny Incest Investigation*. Research studies carried out on case conferences in the UK have indicated that they can be problematic in a number of different areas. Negative influences include stereotyping and poor chairing (Hallett & Stevenson, 1980). A recent study by Hallett (1995) suggests that while participants consider conferences useful, weaknesses and even detrimental factors are acknowledged, with concerns about the wrong people influencing decisions. Mistaken assumptions about the worth of case conferences were identified by Reder, Duncan and Gray (1993) who, in an analysis of child abuse tragedies, offer the view that case conferences, while valuable, can be the objects of unrealistically high expectations. They suggest that the processes involved are by no means straightforward.

Data from Phase One indicates that one quarter of child abuse notifications in the South Eastern Health Board are subject to case conferences, a finding which is consistent with British studies (Farmer & Owen, 1995; Gibbons, Conroy & Bell, 1995). While we did not have the opportunity to observe the case conference process in action during this study, we did use the opportunity to examine the views of practitioners about the usefulness or otherwise of their role and function in the child protection system. Although case conferences were not held on each of the sampled cases during this particular period, all the professionals interviewed had attended more than one case conference within the recent past (either concerning the cases under study or others), and their responses to us were informed by their experiences at those meetings.

We asked respondents for their views and experiences of case conferences with regard to the following areas: role and function of case conferences; the interactional processes; decision making; sharing of responsibility; and follow up. We also invited them to discuss their views on parental participation at case conferences.

THE ROLE AND FUNCTION OF CASE CONFERENCES IN THE CHILD PROTECTION SYSTEM

We found very strong support for the position of case conferences in both the early and later stages of investigation and longer term management of child abuse cases. Practitioners valued the way that the meetings enabled the sharing of information and facilitated planning. Case conferences were seen as helpful in 'making joint decisions,' providing a comprehensive social history of the family, 'clarifying roles', hearing 'different angles' from the various participants, and in helping 'to focus things every so often'.

Social workers in particular suggested another positive function of these inter-agency meetings, namely the 'sharing of responsibility'. The frequency with which this was mentioned emphasised its obvious importance to them. The case conference was seen by the social workers as a forum for highlighting 'that other professionals have a role to play in child protection' and that 'by clarifying roles and giving information not already known, responsibility can be shared'. Some social workers clearly felt isolated at times and found the case conferences useful 'particularly when you are working on your own, it's a good way of sharing responsibility'.

Case conferences are clearly time-consuming and expensive exercises, and there were mixed views as to whether there were enough, or too many of them. The majority view appeared to be in favour of holding them frequently; in fact, one practitioner commented that 'it should be possible to have case conferences more often, at present you really need a good reason to get one'. However, the point was made that, on occasions, holding a case confer-

ence can be a superfluous measure, and, in at least one case, a social worker felt that the meeting was held, not in the interests of
the children and family, but for the sake of the professionals.

> There were elements of keeping [themselves] covered, when
> the same end could have been achieved by talking to the
> mother without a case conference at all.

Other practitioners mentioned the difficulty in setting them up,
given the pressure that most workers are under. Invitations were
not always positively received, and as a social worker said: 'you
can feel like a flea in the ear of other professionals' in trying to get
them to find a suitable time.

THE CASE CONFERENCE PROCESS

It was generally observed that case conferences ran more
smoothly and efficiently when participants came prepared, and
where the attending professionals were all necessary to the discussion, rather than being invited routinely. Practitioners generally considered that the meetings they had attended were well
chaired, and that the contributions of all participants were both
heard and valued. There was also agreement that roles were well
understood and appreciated, and there was little evidence of inter-agency or inter-professional tensions dominating the proceedings.

A minority of professionals who were interviewed were critical
of the discussion process at case conferences which they had attended, in which, according to a social worker:

> . . . not enough attention is paid to clients' social contexts,
> and there is too much emphasis on personal opinion . . .
> judgements are made without criteria being made explicit.

It was also suggested that 'personal opinions' and 'hearsay' determined some contributions. The tendency to 'sit and talk' or
turn the meetings into 'talking shops' was also highlighted by
both a teacher and a social worker. Prolonged discussion was seen
by other workers to shorten the time available for planning, so
that there was a 'tendency to rush through issues' and 'decisions
are made hurriedly'.

DECISION-MAKING AT CASE CONFERENCES

The importance and usefulness of the case conference as a 'decision making forum' was emphasised by most professionals, but there was a view, voiced by a number of social workers, that some of the plans made were quite impractical, and failed to acknowledge the limits of what could be achieved. Social workers felt that 'case conferences need to be focused on realistic decision making' rather than what was currently happening, where 'it's as if whatever they [the other professionals] suggested, the social worker could go off and find it without any difficulties'. They were critical of the high expectation that social workers automatically rectify situations 'as if a social worker visiting is the answer to all child abuse'.

Other factors seen to influence decision making included the availability of resources and legal constraints. Lack of suitable placements in certain situations and inadequate grounds for taking court orders inevitably limited the ability of the conference to make suitable plans. In a minority of cases, practitioners considered that the presence of these factors caused plans to be constructed on the basis of what was possible, rather than what was needed.

SHARING RESPONSIBILITY

Despite their belief that case conferences can serve to 'share responsibility' between the different participants, social workers complained that this did not always happen. One social worker was critical of the lack of preparedness of the other participants:

> . . . what happens is that people come along, but even though they're all supposed to have reports, only the social workers have . . . there isn't a sharing of responsibility.

There was a perception among some social workers that they were 'left carrying it all' and a feeling that, even though other professionals engaged in discussion, 'it's like a paper exercise . . . it's all being minuted and it's grand, but you're still left with the headache'. Others highlighted the need to address the 'automatic assumptions that are made that the social worker will do all the work'. This issue was also remarked on by a social worker outside Community Care, who noticed that, despite the intensity of inter-professional involvement at the case conference, 'the responsibility falls back on the Community Care social worker who is left to bring the bad tidings back to the client'.

FOLLOW-UP TO CASE CONFERENCES

The need to tighten up review arrangements after case conferences was noted by a public health nurse, who pointed to the risk that 'everyone gets on and does their own part of the work'. She felt that case conferences should be pro-active as well as reactive and 'are pointless if they are just used to deal with crises'. A social worker was also critical of the lack of follow-up from other practitioners, and felt 'it's like the case winds down' once the case conference is dispersed.

PARENTAL PARTICIPATION AT CASE CONFERENCES

There are no specific norms with regard to parental attendance in the region, although in some cases parents do attend for part of the case conference. In the cases we sampled, there were very few examples of this, and there was no situation in which parents engaged in any part of the decision making process, or attended the whole case conference. Findings from Phase One of the study indicate that parents attended for some part of only 4 per cent of case conferences held during the study period. Parental attendance is an issue which has received some attention both in inquiry reports (McGuinness, 1993; Keenan, 1996) and in the new Garda notification guidelines (Department of Health, 1995). We took the opportunity to ask the child protection practitioners whom we interviewed for their views about parents attending case conferences, and how they thought it might be best managed.

There was general agreement amongst the professionals that parents should be invited to attend at least some part of any case conference which discussed them and their children, with some reservations from teachers, who tended to feel the matter should be decided on a case by case basis. Most practitioners expressed the view that parents were 'entitled to have their say' and should be given an opportunity 'to defuse their powerlessness'. One worker felt that if parents came to these meetings 'it could control the gossip, and people would be more careful of what they would say'. The reasons given in favour of their participation included the possibility that, having witnessed the concern of all of the professionals who met, parents might 'take the issue more seriously'. Social workers felt that parents could then see that decisions and views for their children's protection and welfare were from a team, rather than from individuals.

Views were more mixed, however, on the type of participation envisaged. The majority of those interviewed felt that parents should not attend the whole conference. Some suggested that they attend 'before the decision is made' and have some part in the discussion, and others felt they should just come in at the end. Views also varied as to whether parents should meet all, or only a small number, of the case conference participants, some believing that parents would be overwhelmed by meeting all the professionals who had been present. A public health nurse expressed her preference for leaving a case conference before the mother came in, wanting 'to remain neutral in her eyes'.

Those who preferred only partial attendance expressed concern about the intimidating nature of a large meeting, and the fact that it might seem 'like a trial or inquisition' for the client. The other main reason given for excluding parents from the whole meeting was the inhibiting effect their presence would have on the professionals, 'people would not be able to say what they think' and could 'lose some important insights'. It was felt that parents might misunderstand the process where 'professionals need to battle out the issues' and interpret the discussion process as 'confusion among the professionals about the case'. One practitioner said:

> . . . professionals might be talking about a situation but the ordinary person's impression of it could be taken or seen as a value judgement . . . professionals talk in a language that many clients don't understand.

The views of parents themselves on whether or not they should be present at case conferences are reported fully in the next chapter. It is appropriate at this point, however, to note that their opinions contrasted sharply with those of the professionals.

A minority of practitioners felt strongly that parents should attend the whole case conference. One child care worker expressed the view about a case she was involved in: 'It was sad to see so many people deciding about other people's lives . . . the mother should have been there'. A social worker who had worked in another agency where full parental and child attendance was the norm had found it quite manageable. There was agreement that different arrangements should exist in some circumstances, e.g. if the parent was a sexual abuse perpetrator, or if parents were separated.

The need for training before parental participation could be introduced as a policy was stressed, and also the need to make 'time available for parents to be prepared'. It was felt that the Health Boards 'would need to make a commitment to the notion' in order to properly establish it as a policy. In general, however, there was no strong opposition to the idea, and there was acknowledgement of the need to recognise the important role played by parents and the importance of their involvement when serious decisions were being made.

CONCLUSION

To conclude, case conferences were seen as important in terms of sharing information, making plans and sharing responsibility for cases amongst the different professionals. There were a few reservations about their efficacy, given their time-consuming nature and the difficulty in getting personnel to attend. Criticisms about the process of discussion and decision making included too much concentration on hearsay and personal opinion, a tendency to rush decision making, and the unrealistic nature of some plans which were suggested. Several social workers were critical, once again, of the way their own profession was left with the burden of responsibility once the meeting was over.

Parental participation at case conferences was encouraged by most professionals, but only to a very limited degree, and it was suggested that any plans to introduce parental attendance should be preceded by training for all professionals in the context of a strong commitment to this ideal by the Health Boards. It would be the view of the researchers, however, that such a step should not be taken without serious consideration of the implications for all concerned. Reference to some British research confirms the sensitive issues involved. Although the commitment to full case conference attendance by parents is unequivocal in British guidance, and is, in general, supported in the research, many problems have been associated with it. Research by Farmer and Owen (1995), Thoburn, Lewis and Shemmings (1995) and Cleaver and Freeman (1995) highlight the misunderstandings, confusion and pain that can be experienced by parents who are not fully prepared, and who believe that they are at the meetings to listen and be admonished rather than participate in decision making. As Corby, Millar and Young (1996) point out, an undeniable power differential exists between carers and professionals, and unless this is explicitly acknowledged, parents may perceive that it is their 'compliance' rather than their 'openness' that is valued. They postulate that a level of disagreement can be quite constructive, and should even be encouraged, provided it is properly handled.

Our findings suggest that the practice of inviting parents to attend for a portion, but not all, of the meetings is currently operated in parts of the region. Again, we would have some reservations about this, which are confirmed by other research. The studies by Farmer and Owen, and Thoburn *et al.* agree that the negative effects experienced by parents tend to be exacerbated if they are partially excluded, and the 'closed door' experience of waiting outside a meeting can cause them more feelings of anger, resentment, and punishment. However, not only the parents' anxiety, but also professional anxiety about full participation needs to be addressed. Whilst strongly endorsing the practitioners' and the parents' aspirations towards greater openness and eventual full participation, we would suggest that this is not attempted without careful preparation and training.[1]

It is timely, at this point, to move on to the issue of parental involvement in child protection work. The following section will deal firstly with the perceptions of social workers on their ability to work in 'partnership', to be followed by the perspectives of parents themselves.

---

[1] A protocol for the conduct of case conferences has been produced by the Southern Health Board (1997) which includes preparation and procedures for the attendance of parents and children.

CHAPTER SIX

PARENTAL INVOLVEMENT IN CASES OF
CHILD ABUSE AND NEGLECT

INTRODUCTION

A considerable amount of attention has been given in British research to the importance of parental perspectives in child protection work. The notion of partnership with parents has been heavily emphasised in the UK *Children Act, 1989*. Likewise, the Irish
Child Care Act, 1991 reinforces the aspiration towards working
with families in their own homes, and involving parents in the
construction of child care plans. Child abuse guidelines in Ireland
assert the importance of keeping parents informed of any actions,
and including them, where possible, in the construction of plans.
The positive impact of parental involvement on child protection
outcomes is affirmed in the literature (Thoburn, Lewis & Shemmings, 1995; Cleaver & Freeman, 1995), and it is generally recognised that practice should move in the direction of sharing as
much of the decision making as possible with parents.

To begin this section we will again refer back to Phase One,
where we found that, in many instances, parents were not actively
involved in the child protection process. Only a very small proportion of parents had any level of involvement in case conferences held about their family. This is despite the finding that most
children subject to alleged or actual abuse or neglect continue to
be cared for in their own homes.

The data on which the first part of this chapter is based emanated from interviews with social workers. They were specifically
asked about partnership with parents in the context of longer
term casework. Later in the chapter, we will discuss the findings
from interviews with parents from the eighteen sample cases, who
were invited to give their views on the investigation, on the level

of risk they thought their child was under at the time of the investigation, and the on-going management of the case. They were also asked about the involvement of the Gardaí with their families. In addition, parents were asked about their attitude to the kind of service they received, their involvement with the child protection service of the Health Board, and their perceptions of the level of partnership they experienced with professionals. Parents' views on case conferences were also sought, and, finally, we asked them about their perceptions of the present situation for both their children and themselves.

SECTION ONE: SOCIAL WORKERS' PERCEPTIONS OF PARTNERSHIP WITH PARENTS IN CHILD PROTECTION WORK: PARENTS' INVOLVEMENT IN THE CONSTRUCTION OF THE CHILD PROTECTION PLAN

Social workers reported that, in the majority of the cases studied, the child protection plan was negotiated with at least one parent. There were three exceptions to this: in two instances, both cases of extra familial abuse, the parents declined to have any contact with the Health Boards and, in the third, the social worker currently involved was relatively new and was unclear about early parental involvement.

Where parents were not involved in negotiating the child protection plan, they were informed about it after the case conference. There were a few instances where parents were unhappy about the plan which was envisaged, but did agree to comply with it. For example, one mother did not believe her child's allegation of child sexual abuse by her father, but still went along with the Health Board's referral to the child sexual abuse assessment unit. In other instances, only certain elements of the plan were shared with parents; for example, one mother was not told about the involvement of the Gardaí in the investigation of her child's disclosure of sexual abuse.

In summary, it appears that, in most instances, at least one parent was involved in the construction of child protection plans, whether they were totally in agreement with these plans or not. Where parents were not involved, this was generally due to parental refusal to co-operate.

RELATIONSHIPS BETWEEN SOCIAL WORKERS AND PARENTS

Social workers reported that the frequency of their contact with families in the sample varied, depending on the nature of the cases. Contact happened primarily on a weekly or fortnightly basis. In a few cases it was monthly, and, in a minority of cases, there was either very little, or no contact at all. One example of where there was no contact concerned a family who refused to deal with the Health Board, and liaison was maintained with the child through the school. In another two instances, contact had ceased because the social workers' attempts to meet the family had failed to elicit any response. In these cases, the social workers did state that other cases took priority and if they had had more time, the families would have been followed up more actively. In some cases, contact with the families had ceased because it had been decided that a more appropriate course of action would be for the social worker to liaise with the relevant services already involved with the families.

The nature of contact between social worker and clients was also examined. Where social workers had regular contact, it was primarily with the main carer in the household. In the sample under study, this was most often lone female or male parents. Where relevant, social workers also had ongoing involvement with the non-resident parents of the household, generally about access issues. In most cases, especially where the children were older, children and their respective parents were seen together for at least some of the visits. In nearly half of the cases, the social workers saw the children on their own.

Few definitive statements were offered by the social workers as to whether their relationships with families were good or bad *per se*. Rather, the responses comprised a range of impressions about the nature of the relationships. Furthermore, as one would expect, the nature of the relationships changed over the nine months covered in the study.

A few social workers did describe their relationship with all the family members as being mainly positive. One worker, who had been involved with the family from the outset, described the relationship with both mother and children as 'very good and is progressing very well . . . I don't see any problems at the moment.'

The opposite applied in a few other instances, where social workers described their relationships with parents as particularly difficult. One worker described her contact with a mother as 'very poor . . . mother is reluctant to meet with me and it is a real struggle with her'. Another practitioner described her contact with both parents as 'resistant and antagonistic', while another referred to her relationship with a father as 'very stormy'. The latter social worker claimed that despite the fact that it had been the father who had brought the child care concerns to the attention of the Health Board in the first place, he had been 'very uncooperative and constantly problematic'.

However, it was more common for social workers to report mixed versions of their relationships with families. Furthermore, in a number of cases, the nature of the relationship varied according to which family member they were discussing.

A key issue for most workers was the balance between their authoritative child protection role and their attempts to build a supportive relationship with parents and/or children. For example one worker reported that:

> I get on well with mother, she feels she gets listened to when she needs it but I pose a threat to her still . . . sometimes the authoritative role goes against the grain.

Another described her relationship with a mother as being good and supportive in relation to the sexual abuse of her child but 'I get the sense that she sees the Health Board as intruding, and would prefer if there was no contact from them at all'. Conflicts also arose in relation to direct work with children, where they sometimes found it hard to build trusting relationships due to their parents' resistance to the social workers.

Lack of trust in the Health Board influenced parents at times. The social worker in one case reported that a father was so mistrustful of her as a representative of the Health Board that she found him personally threatening. Memories of negative experiences with the Health Board interfered with some clients' ability to engage with social workers. One worker reported that the mother:

... was initially reluctant to have social work intervention, she had a negative experience with a social worker in the past and this really affected our work ... things are improving now though ...

Similarly, another social worker reported difficulty in working with a child who 'generally felt negatively towards social workers ... she felt let down and badly treated ...'

A number of social workers reported how a conflict of interest between separated partners, or between parents and children, affected their relationship with families. For example, a worker described her relationship with the estranged father of a child as good and that he was 'one hundred percent co-operative', but felt that this was more to do with his concern to get custody of the children than his overt willingness to work with the Health Board. In a number of cases, parent-child difficulties seemed to create tension which permeated their relationship with the social worker. For example, one worker described her relationship with the child as good but strained because the child was 'torn between her parents', and therefore was having difficulties 'being open with the social worker'. In another case, the parents refused to have any contact with the social worker, but contact with the child was continued, at her own request. In another instance, the relationship between the social worker and a mother was directly affected by the fact that the mother was dismissive of the child's allegations, and did not want Health Board involvement. She had 'actively tried to dissuade the child' from being involved with the social work service.

In some cases, personal circumstances or characteristics appeared to influence relationships. One social worker described her relationship with a mother as good but 'limited', due to the mother's mental health problems. Another practitioner described a mother as 'difficult to engage ... with limited insight into the child's problems', while another reported that it was necessary to be 'formal and firm' with a father, in order to get him to take the issues seriously.

In some instances, the parent who was the alleged offender was uncooperative, for example where a father had been accused of child sexual abuse in the past, he and his wife refused to work with the Health Board. However, this was not necessarily, or indeed usually, the case. For example, in a physical abuse case, where the mother's partner was the alleged abuser, the social worker described her relationship with him in quite positive terms. She described how he admitted to the allegations and co-operated with the investigation. Furthermore, according to the social worker, he showed more insight into the children's needs than their mother had and had responsibly taken on the role of parenting and disciplining within the household. Likewise in a sexual abuse case, where a father was the alleged abuser, the social worker described her relationship with him as 'fairly open . . . relaxed . . .' She conceded that:

> . . . following the allegation of child sexual abuse relations were strained . . . there was a loss of trust and anger . . . but I think we have worked through this now and he [father] has been able to move on with the work with the child and the social worker.

Some social workers found children 'wary' of them initially, but the majority described their long term relationships with children as trusting and positive.

PARTNERSHIP WITH PARENTS

In order to further explore the nature of relationships with families, we asked social workers for their perceptions of the effect of investigation on families, and then asked them for their views on partnership with families in the longer term.

The increasing emphasis of Community Care social work on child protection investigation was identified by one worker as having a 'wholly negative impact on our ability to work in partnership with parents'. Another social worker queried the actual feasibility of the task, asking 'how close can you come to partnership with parents within such an unequal relationship?' In a number of cases, respondents were aware of the controlling nature of their child protection mandate. One practitioner reflected that while she could 'claim' to be working in partnership with a particular parent, she was also very aware that she held a high level of control over him: 'he was particularly co-operative, but had been advised to do that by his solicitor . . . it's difficult to define this as partnership'.

The majority of social workers considered themselves to be working in partnership with families in the longer term, at least to some extent, yet they demonstrated variance as to the extent of such partnership and a number of respondents found the meaning of the concept problematic.

Key indicators of partnership were identified as being, firstly, where the social worker considered herself as an advocate for the client, for example in negotiation with another agency, as described here:

> . . . there have been a lot of meetings with the housing department where the mother sees me as a mediator for her . . . as an ally . . . she has found it less threatening to deal with the housing department since I became involved.

Secondly, partnership was seen in terms of joint decision making: 'decisions are made in conjunction with the mother . . . we worked together to sort out other problems'; and thirdly, in terms of 'ongoing communication between worker, mother and child'.

It was not unusual for practitioners to report that they were working in partnership with only certain members of the family. For example, one worker felt she could work co-operatively with a mother and child, but found the father mistrustful and hostile to the Health Board because of allegations which had been made against him. Likewise, another practitioner claimed that while she had been able to work with the father and children: 'it has been difficult with the mother because she is manipulative and resistant to social work intervention'. In two other cases, the social workers felt they were working in partnership with the children, but not their parents.

In summary, we found that social workers generally had regular contact with their clients. Where there was no contact, this was sometimes for a pragmatic reason, such as parental refusal to be involved or the active involvement of other services at the time. There was also a minority of cases where absence of contact had been due to scarcity of time on the part of the social workers, and was accidental rather then planned. There was a small number of cases where relationships between social workers and families were defined as either 'good' or 'poor'. However, in most instances, assessment of relationships was mixed, due to a whole range of factors, the principal among which were:

- the personal rapport between the social worker and client;

- the client's past experience of the Health Board and of social workers;

- internal issues such as conflicts within families or individuals' different interests in maintaining co-operative relationships.

Social workers reported varied perceptions of their ability to work in partnership with families. They found that partnership was more difficult to achieve in initial stages of investigation, but as they became more involved with the families in the longer term, it appeared to become easier.

Given the range and complexity of relationships between social workers and clients, it is all the more relevant and important for a study such as this to reflect the views of 'consumers' of the service. With the above findings in mind, we sought to interview as many as possible of the parents in the eighteen sample cases.

SECTION TWO: THE PARENTS' PERSPECTIVE

Meetings with the parents were negotiated for the most part by their social workers, who gave them letters from the researchers inviting them to participate in the study. The fact that fourteen out of the eighteen sets of parents agreed to meet us bears testimony to their desire to have as much involvement as possible in child protection activities related to their children. Four sets of parents were not interviewed. One had declined our request and the social workers chose not to approach the other three because they felt the experience would be stressful for them.

The cases involved in this phase of the study consisted of:

- six sexual abuse cases;

- two sexual abuse/neglect cases;

- two sexual abuse/physical abuse cases;

- two physical abuse cases; and

- two neglect cases.

There were eight female lone parents, three of whom were alleged to have physically abused or neglected their children, and five whose children had been abused by their ex-partners.

Three other lone parents were male, two of whom were alleged to have sexually abused their daughters, and one whose parenting skills were not considered adequate and whose daughter had been abused by someone outside the family.

The group also included three cohabiting couples, one of which was jointly involved in an allegation of neglect and sexual abuse, and in another case, the male cohabitee was alleged to have physically abused a child.

In the third two-parent situation, the identity of the alleged abuser was not known, though the male cohabitee had been suspected initially.

Parents' Views of the Initial Child Protection Investigation

It is important to note that in just over half (nine) of these situations, the incident or concern which led to the investigation was alleged to have been committed by somebody outside the immediate household, including two cases where the alleged abuser left the family home around the time the child abuse concern came to attention.

The parents whom we interviewed who allegedly abused their children included the three lone male parents, two of whom were suspected of sexually abusing their children, and one who was judged to have poor parenting skills. In the three 'cohabiting' situations (where we interviewed the female partners, according to the arrangements made between the social workers and the families), there were allegations of physical abuse against the children's common-law stepfather, in one instance. In the second case, there were suspicions of sexual abuse by the child's father, and neglect by both parents. In the third case, the perpetrator of sexual abuse was unknown, though there was initial suspicion that it was the cohabitee.

Three female lone parents were interviewed; one had hit her daughter; and the two others had been found neglectful of their children by the Health Board.

Farmer and Owen (1995) found in their British study that when the views of parents and child protection workers were conjoined, the experience of being investigated was less traumatic. The reactions of parents whom we interviewed in this study were very similar. Three of the parents who had been investigated for abuse found the process reasonably satisfactory, linked to their own certainty that they had not perpetrated the abuse. One of them, a single father whose ex-partner accused him of sexually abusing his daughter, had worked in a hospital setting 'and knew about what social workers do'. He said that they were 'helpful' at the time of their initial contact with him. He did express frustration, however, that the social workers 'were accepting all the allegations and believing them' without 'being properly investigated'.

A mother whose partner had been accused of sexually abusing their daughter, and who was deemed by the Health Board to be living in very unsatisfactory accommodation, said she found the investigation 'okay', but did not consider it at all necessary. Another mother, whose partner had initially been suspected of sexual abuse, found the investigation constructive, particularly as she did not believe her partner was guilty. She was anxious to find out who had abused her daughter and found the social worker 'good, very understanding, very helpful'. She was not happy that all her children had to be assessed for possible sexual abuse, but felt obliged to concede: 'I was annoyed that the rest of the children had to go . . . but I let them go'.

The other parents who were being investigated themselves were less happy about the process. Two were slightly less resentful of it than others.

One woman had hit her daughter, but the main thrust of the investigation was around previous sexual abuse by her partner. She eventually conceded that the investigation was inevitable:

> . . . no one likes social workers calling to their doors or having anything to do with them . . . but I realised there

must be a big problem if the social worker was contacting me.

The other, who had been reportedly leaving her children unsupervised, also came to accept the necessity for some kind of contact: 'I got a terrible shock when the social worker called . . . had no idea what it was for', but she 'accepted that the social worker had to follow through'.

Some other parents were less conciliatory. One woman, also a lone parent, felt very undermined:

> I don't like anyone coming in to tell me how to look after my children . . . I know myself I'm rearing my children all right . . . it was embarrassing, made me feel low.

A male lone parent who was initially investigated for the sexual abuse of his daughter found the process extremely distressing:

> . . . it wasn't very nice . . . it put pressure on everyone . . . I didn't care whether they believed me or not . . . I knew that I did nothing to her . . . it was very serious . . . I was afraid I could be put away for nine or ten years for something I didn't do . . . I was awful scared.

Another lone male parent whose child had been abused by someone else, but whose own parenting skills were very much in doubt, found the investigative process 'awful'. 'I thought they were trying to take [my daughter] away because it [the abuse] was my fault.' The most negative comments about investigation came from a mother whose children had complained that her cohabitee had hit them. She had been part of the conflict which had provoked the assault, though she did not consider it 'abusive'. When the Health Board became involved she:

> . . . felt totally intimidated . . . angry . . . hurt . . . stripped naked . . . I've reared them up to this and now I was being reprimanded for chastising my children . . . I felt the whole business was handled like a court case and I resented having to prove my innocence . . . my family was seen as 'dysfunctional' because I was separated from my husband . . . I thought my kids were going to be taken . . . it's a feeling I'd never want to experience again.

The five remaining parents whom we interviewed were female lone parents who had come to Health Board attention because their children had been abused by their ex-partners. In four cases, discovery of child sexual abuse, some of which included domestic violence, had precipitated their separation. In one, the child had been in the custody of her father until the most recent physical abuse incident and was now living with her mother. Despite the traumatic discovery that their children had been abused, most of the mothers viewed the investigation positively. One said: 'it was a relief to do something and get moving on it . . . the social worker was fine and handled the situation very sensitively'. Three others said they appreciated the contact, and the help that came with it, including, in one case, full-time care for the children. One mother, however, expressed irritation. Her child went into care initially. The mother was desperately worried about her, and found the investigation 'frustrating'. Her daughter had been living with her husband, and she felt she was left with very little information at the beginning: 'it took a long time to get the facts . . . I was frustrated at the lack of power of the social workers and was left feeling annoyed . . .'

In summary, we found that the response of parents to being investigated for alleged child abuse tended to vary according to the circumstances, and according to whether they themselves were implicated in the allegation. While some were resigned to the process, those who were 'accused' found the situation most difficult, fearing that their children would be taken into care, and resenting the intrusion of the child protection workers. A number of mothers whose children had been abused by their ex-partners had found the investigative process to be supportive, despite the trauma involved for both their children and themselves.

Parents' Perception of Risk to Their Children at the Time of the Investigation

Parents' attitudes to investigation, and their likely co-operation with child protection services, depended to some degree on their acceptance that their children were at risk. Evidence from the literature suggests that the process is particularly painful and difficult for non-abusing mothers who have to live with the fact that their children were abused by their cohabitees (Hooper, 1992). The mothers in this study whose children had been abused by their ex-partners appeared, by the time we spoke to them, to have come to terms with what happened, and unanimously agreed that, until the incidents had been discovered and addressed, their children were in dangerous situations; 'They were at risk of molestation'; 'yes . . . from my boyfriend . . . he never liked the children and I was afraid he would hit them'; 'My husband was very cruel to me and the children were affected too . . . it was terrible for me but even more for the children . . .' In one case, the children had been removed to care, and, though the mother was very regretful of this, she openly acknowledged her inability to protect them: 'my husband is not locked up and is still around . . . they're in safe hands now . . . for me, the children come first'.

Some parents whom we spoke to were inclined to minimise the risk their children had been under. Some agreed that their children had been in some danger, but not from any deficits in their own parental care. One mother felt that most of the hazards came from the neighbourhood. Her children were of mixed race and she said: 'they put notes through the door saying they don't want black children in the estate'. Another mother felt that the risk had come from the child's own promiscuous behaviour: 'Yes [she] was at risk, but a lot of it was her own doing'. A lone father agreed his child had been in danger from the man who sexually abused her, but 'not once she said it . . . I'm able to protect her'. Another lone father felt his daughter's welfare suffered: 'not at home . . . she was at risk when she was running away from home to her mother's . . . I don't know what they be doing up in that house . . .' In another situation where a child had run away, she had been placed by the Health Board in 'a hostel for battered women' and it was there that her mother considered her to be at most risk.

A number of parents whom we interviewed, however, did not believe that their children had been at risk at all. The mother whose children had been hit by her cohabitee claimed that the investigation was 'unjustified . . . I wouldn't mind saying that anywhere and would have records to back it up'. A mother who had been reported as leaving her children unsupervised said 'no . . . not at all . . . the accusations that were made were false'. The

fact that her child was still happy living at home was proof
enough for another mother that her father did not sexually abuse
her. The father whose ex-partner had accused him of sexual abuse
denied that his children had been at risk in any way: 'I looked after them as best I could . . . they are much happier now'.

The fact that some of the above quoted parents were unable to
acknowledge the alleged risk to their children which had undoubtedly triggered off the Health Board's involvement illustrates
the difficult context in which child protection workers were operating. The fact that so many practitioners had managed to forge
good working relationships with them reflects the skill and effort
that goes into this type of work.

Parents' Attitudes to Ongoing Involvement of the Child Protection System

Research in the UK (Cleaver & Freeman, 1995) highlights the
impact which the initial investigation has on parents. It was
found to play a significant part in shaping their perspectives, to
the extent that it could help or hinder their ability to work on an
ongoing basis with the services. Ultimately, the outcome for their
children can be affected by parents' openness to interventions.
Cleaver and Freeman showed that the greater the degree of culpability experienced by parents, the lower the level at which they
were prepared to co-operate with the child protection system. In
their view, this highlighted the need for sensitivity in initial investigations.

In this study we found that some parents experienced the child
protection investigative process as very harsh, and very few of
them were able to acknowledge that their ability to provide for
their children's protection and welfare had been in any way defi-
cient at the time of the initial allegation. However, despite the
very difficult context in which contact was initiated between the
child protection system and the families, the majority of them at
this stage, six to nine months onwards, said that their relationship with the Health Board child protection workers was generally satisfactory. In general, the comments about ongoing contact
with the child care services were positive, even from some of the
parents who felt very negative at the outset. One mother who had

felt very intimidated initially said she now regarded the child guidance service she had been offered as 'a lifeline'. Another mother, who was initially shocked at the Health Board's interest in her family, said: 'once I got to know the social worker . . . didn't like her at first . . . now I feel fine about her', and she appreciated the help she got in making links with the Housing Department. A lone male parent who had felt very threatened initially later found the social worker 'fine . . . helpful'.

It is important to consider these findings with care. The parents and social workers interviewed highlighted the lack of choice parents have about their involvement with the child protection services. While parents reported positively about social work involvement, many of the same parents reflected a lack of control over the process, and expressed the view that they would prefer not to have involvement with the child protection agencies in the first place. The parents voiced some reservations and criticisms about the type and quality of the general service offered, and these will be dealt with later. The child protection workers generally managed to sustain useful and constructive relationships with their clients, against considerable odds. It must be acknowledged that the parents who were interviewed agreed to talk to us voluntarily. In that sense they could be judged to be a self-selected group of co-operative clients. Nevertheless, these parents represented approximately three-quarters of the whole sample, their views reflect both positive and negative views, and reliable criteria were used to choose the cases.[1] We therefore consider the inferences made from these data to be quite valid.

Parents' Evaluation of the Services Offered to Them by the Child Protection System

Parents expressed mixed attitudes to the range of services offered to families by the child protection system. In a number of cases where child sexual abuse was suspected, the families were re-

---

[1] i.e. the cases in the sample were those which were notified for child abuse and neglect in the period May–June 1995 and were still open six months later. Of those cases, those which involved the broadest range of other professionals were identified. Cases were proportionately selected from each Community Care area.

ferred to the Child Sexual Abuse Assessment Unit, about which they were quite positive It was judged to have been 'brilliant' and 'very good'; 'the doctor in the unit was very upfront with me'. One mother said that, despite the trauma of the interviews, 'it was a relief to get it out and for the child to be able to talk about it . . . I had a lot of support there'.

Five families who were offered a home help service found this very beneficial. One mother described the person involved as 'like a mother to me and all the kids love her'. She particularly appreciated the regular overnight breaks with which this service provided her.

Where full time care had been provided, in foster families in two cases and in residential centres in two other cases, this was also perceived as helpful, and the quality of foster care in particular was highly praised. One mother was critical of the fact that her daughter was in unsuitable accommodation for quite a while before a place in a hostel for teenagers became available. She also felt that the hostel was 'too comfortable . . . the conditions are twenty times better than we have at home . . . how could I give her what she had there . . .' However both parents whose children had been in residential care were very appreciative of the fact that the residential child care workers still kept in contact with them; 'mind you, the hostel was a great help . . . the best . . . they kept in touch the whole way and were great'. Where Community Care child care workers were involved they were described as 'great'. In the one case where a family centre had been used, it was described by the mother as 'brilliant'.

Some therapeutic services for the children and families were also deemed successful. A mother described how 'the child guidance social worker was able to tease out what the initial problem was . . . which I hadn't been able to do . . . so something I hadn't wanted at first has proved helpful'. A lone father was satisfied both with the quality of counselling his daughter was getting and the speed with which it had been arranged. In another situation the input of a family therapist was greatly valued. Psychology services, though initiated in three cases, had petered out fairly quickly. In one case, the mother was unsure as to why treatment had been terminated, and, in two more, the children themselves had opted out of treatment.

Social work intervention appeared to be valued by parents, particularly where it involved direct work with children. A father described how the social worker would come and 'take the child out and talk to her, and the child was able to talk to her . . . she would come back quite happy and contented'. Another father reported that the social worker 'visits the children more often now than before [his daughter] made those allegations and that's good . . . like, the visits are good for them I think . . .'

One mother, who said she would 'prefer if none of them came to my door', acknowledged that:

> . . . the social worker is helpful, she finds out information for me . . . I can talk to her . . . she's the first person I'll go to . . . I'd go to her before I'd go to my own mother.

Another mother was appreciative of the response she gets from the social worker:

> . . . if I have a problem I'll just ring [the social worker] no matter what it is, housing or anything, information, anything I might need, and she comes out to me.

In a couple of instances, parents were critical of the Health Board's failure to pay due attention to situations that the parents themselves felt were risky. A mother whose child had been physically abused by her husband while in his custody was concerned about the safety of the other children in that household. She had been told that the social worker had limited powers of entry to his home, but was frustrated by it.

> I know the man . . . I really want a social worker to get into that house but it isn't happening . . . I'm not happy with the way those children are not being supervised.

In another situation, a mother whose child had been, in her words, 'molested' by an older child in the neighbourhood was unhappy that 'the Health Board didn't do anything'.

Criticisms included 'gaps' in contact, e.g. when a child moved from one placement to another 'the social worker stopped visiting'. In another situation, the social worker had left but in the six months since her replacement had come, the mother had not received any contact. This was quite problematic for herself and her family, as the rest of the services which had been set up also ground to a halt. A lone father who had found a home help service very beneficial was 'nearly a year without a home help . . . one left and they were supposed to organise another one . . .' Another perceived 'gap' was the lack of services specifically for the parents, which will be dealt with later in this section.

Parents' Views of Garda Involvement in Child Abuse Investigations

This study was based on child abuse referrals which were reported to the Health Board in the very early stages of the implementation of the guidelines for *Notification of Suspected Cases of Child Abuse between the Gardaí and Health Boards* (Department of Health, 1995). Data from Phase One of the study would suggest that the notification procedures were not fully operational at the time, but it appears that there was Garda involvement in the majority of cases which we sampled, and most of the parents we interviewed had contact with the Gardaí during the course of the investigation.

Some parents found the involvement of the Gardaí very helpful, particularly when they felt the situation was being handled sensitively:

> We knew the Garda as he was local . . . liked him . . . found him easy to talk to . . . he always wore plain clothes . . . encouraged her to make a statement but gave her a lot of time and space to decide for herself what to do . . . he was very professional.

Another parent found the Gardaí she met 'helpful . . . had both male and female Gardaí . . . preferred the female . . . easier to talk to and more helpful'.

However, most parents' perceptions of Garda involvement in child abuse investigations were less positive. In some cases, parents were disappointed at the lack of follow-up, or feedback from investigations. One mother described her frustration at the Gardaí because of their failure to interview her husband, who was suspected of abusing their daughter:

> . . . they are saying there is nothing more they can do until father comes to talk to them . . . he is refusing to do this . . . it shouldn't be left up to him to go down . . . they should come up . . . he should be questioned and then I would know one way or the other.

Another mother in the same situation had asked, for her own safety, for the Gardaí to inform her when they were arresting her husband, 'because I was ready to run . . . but the first I heard was when he rang me himself to tell me'. She had had 'no word' on progress in the case for over three months:

> . . . he [the sergeant] has my phone number, and could ring me once a month even . . . I would like the child to be able to get on with her life . . . it's very daunting for her . . . I would have liked to have the opinion of the sergeant, I got no updates or anything.

Similarly, another mother, whose husband was due to be prosecuted for child sexual abuse, was frustrated with both the lack of action by the Gardaí and the lack of communication from them:

> It's taking so long . . . dragging on . . . you don't get answers, you get cut off . . . they are trying to avoid you . . . no one available when you phone . . .

One of the mothers quoted above was alarmed by what she perceived as false security being offered by a garda to her daughter:

> My only qualms were that the garda said there was no way my husband would go near her and she was guaranteed safety . . . but we found out different once those interviews were done with . . . he could come out whenever he wanted to . . . just walked in, he assaulted her and abused us. We were terrified of him, not safe in our own home. It was worse for her [the child].

Lack of interest by the Gardaí in domestic violence caused some mothers to be critical. One woman talked of her previous experiences: 'When I was being battered by my husband I found them useless'. Another spoke of their slowness to respond in this type of situation:

> Once when he was beating me I sent her [daughter] to a neighbour to ring the police . . . the child was hysterical . . . and it took them an hour and a half to come. They would never rush to your door . . . it made [the child] really insecure then.

Some of the contacts they had with gardaí were also perceived by parents as being insensitive. One mother described how they had arrived late at night to interview her twelve-year-old daughter about an alleged sexual assault:

> They came at 9.45, to my mother's house, and wanted to interview [child]. We didn't let them. They came back and she talked to them. This was after she had been through Ardkeen [hospital]. They came another time, five months after the previous interview and wanted another interview . . . we refused to let her talk to them then and we had to sign a statement to say we wouldn't co-operate . . . we just wanted it dropped then . . .

Another mother described a situation where someone had maliciously reported her to the Gardaí, saying that she had left the children alone in the house. A Garda called and, finding a babysitter, according to the mother:

> . . . went upstairs and started searching around my bedroom . . . when I phoned up the next day, they didn't know what I was talking about.

This woman was known to the Gardaí, and felt that she was being harassed by them.

A lone father was critical of the way he was 'always being stopped' by the Gardaí, who knew there had been concerns about his daughter: 'Any time I'm out they stop me and say "who's minding the young one?" . . .'

Some parents felt that the problem of insensitivity would be overcome if there were particular officers assigned to child abuse work. One mother whose initial contact with the Gardaí was positive, reported a second incident:

> . . . but didn't find them so helpful . . . the reason could have been that the first lot probably had a special interest, and were specialists in the job . . . it's better to deal with a special Garda, it's difficult when dealing with different Gardaí all the time.

Another parent felt that only particular Gardaí should do this type of work:

> You need a specialist . . . one time a different chap came, he was so insensitive he really frightened her . . . shouldn't be involved with kids . . . I didn't like their attitude, the way they 'bulled' in and spoke to people.

In summary, while some parents were pleased and satisfied with the interventions of the Gardaí, others voiced frustration about the lack of communication from them following initial investigative activity, their inadequate response to domestic violence incidents, and perceived insensitivity about the way they carried out their work. Some parents suggested that better outcomes would result from the appointment of specialist Gardaí to deal with child protection issues.

Partnership with Parents

Some parents felt very vulnerable in relation to the way in which information about themselves and their families was treated. For example, a father was aware that his ex-partner was making allegations against him, and that information was sought by the Health Board from the area where he had previously lived. He was frustrated at not having access to this information:

> . . . closed doors . . . that's the way I see it . . . I show all the letters I get but they won't share anything with me . . . what good is it if I have anything to hide . . . the book is opened, no matter what is stated in those letters.

One separated mother was upset because allegations that her partner had abused her children were first discussed with her ex-husband:

> The social worker visited without telling me . . . I'm the parent yet they're contacting him . . . I've reared them . . . this gave my husband something against me and he still uses it as a threat to the girls, uses it as a weapon . . . they shouldn't have that fear but their father was given the weapon by the way the Health Board had handled the case . . .

Another parent felt 'you always feel they're not telling you everything' and a lone father felt that 'social workers are always discussing me and [child] . . . because I'm a single man . . . they would prefer me to have a woman'. Another lone father's grievance centred around what he perceived as a lack of choice about social work involvement:

> I know they have to be looked after well but I'd do it myself anyway . . . it's not as if I wouldn't just because the social worker wasn't calling . . . but I have no choice about them calling . . . they have a right to call at any time, I know that . . . I have no choice about that, but in the end it's myself who has to take care of the children . . . their mother is long gone.

A mother, whose previous partner had abused her children, had a good relationship with all the workers involved, but was a bit irritated that 'when I ask for something, they discuss it with the home help, not me . . . but I'm the one who's asking'.

Another mother expressed annoyance about the way she was treated by residential staff when her daughter was in care. She claimed that arrangements were made for her child, for example, to go on outings, without the mother's knowledge or consent, but felt the situation improved greatly once she made her feelings known:

> I should have been more involved in the first hostel . . . I felt like a visitor when I called instead of her mother . . . the people there acted like they were her mother . . . I didn't know about the transfer from one hostel to another . . . I

should have been involved . . . also she would often be gone places on day trips and things and they'd never let me know . . . I'd ring up to give her a message or to call and they'd tell me she was here and there and I'd know nothing . . . but I told them I wasn't happy about this and then they used to let me know all of the time after that . . . and the hostel did support her coming home, they really did help with that.

A lone father, who now had custody of his daughter, complained about the lack of feedback from the social worker about the original sexual abuse allegation made against him:

. . . once I was asked about them by the doctor and the two social workers I heard nothing more . . . I still don't know today what they think . . . I should know at least whether they believe me or not now . . . I had a right to know . . . [child] was seen in that place . . . the children's centre . . . I wasn't asked to go . . . I know they were asking about the allegations . . . I don't know what came out of it . . . I don't think I heard anything about it . . . like, no one told me what everyone was thinking . . . if they thought I did it or not . . . but I know I didn't and I can't make anyone else believe me.

Another male parent felt he was not trusted, and that the social workers were only waiting for a problem to emerge:

What I feel like is – that the social workers are waiting for me to do something wrong . . . I'm waiting for someone to jump on me and say 'we knew it was going on'. Because I'm a man and [child] is a girl. They think I'll be molesting my daughter.

The above findings indicate a certain amount of resentment on the part of parents regarding their lack of involvement in decision making and planning for their children, and the lack of trust they perceive from the social workers. One forum which has the potential to facilitate partnership would be the inter-agency case conference. We sought parents' views on their participation at such meetings.

Parents' Views on Participation at Case Conferences

The majority of the parents whom we interviewed said, when asked, that they did not know what a case conference was. After the meaning of the term was explained to them, some of the parents realised that, in fact, such meetings had already been held in relation to their families, but they had not been aware of what they were called, or their significance in the child protection system.

Three of the parents whom we spoke to had attended the latter part of case conferences. None of them were particularly happy about this, and two of them, both lone parents, said they would have preferred to be at the whole meeting instead. One of mothers, whose parenting skills had been in question, felt she had a right to hear it all:

> A parent should know what social workers and doctors and whatever were saying . . . they were talking about my family . . . I had a right to be there . . . even if it was just to sit down and listen and tell them what I had to say . . .

Another lone parent, whose ex-partner had abused her daughter, said:

> All of it . . . I felt like after all the interviews, I would have felt better knowing what they had to say, got everybody's opinion on it . . . the doctor in the unit was very upfront with me . . . but at the case conference everything is behind closed doors and you wonder what they're saying and you're very unsure of yourself going in there . . . they should have been more upfront. I should have been more involved, I had never even met the health nurse, I didn't know half of them. Some had already left, names didn't mean anything to me but I would have liked to have their opinions or how they were involved . . . I didn't feel trusted, even though it wasn't me who abused her.

A single father, whose daughter had alleged sexual abuse but later retracted it, was unsure whether or not full attendance at the case conference would have been better for him, as he felt he was already 'judged':

> Well I don't think it would have made any difference to be
> at all of it . . . if they thought I did it, I can't change their
> minds . . . what can I say . . . why would they believe me . . .
> I said what was the truth and I don't know if they believed
> me or not . . .

The reason for this man's pessimism was that he felt quite stig-
matised by the doctor's mention of a previous incident, where he
had been involved with the Gardaí about a matter which was of
no relevance to the current situation:

> Well I was brought in . . . told to sit down and they told me
> what [his daughter] had said . . . asked me did I or did I not
> do it . . . then the doctor said the Gardaí might or might not
> be contacted . . . and then she brought up the thing about a
> criminal record in 1982 . . . she shouldn't have done that . . .
> that's all I heard . . . I heard absolutely no more about it . . .
> I should have heard what had happened . . . it's still hang-
> ing over me.

The feeling of culpability was shared by the other two parents
who had attended the end of the case conferences. One said:

> They made me feel it was my fault . . . that I deserved it . . .
> they weren't listening to me . . . I wasn't getting across to
> them . . .

The other mother also found the process uncomfortable:

> . . . terribly unnerving . . . they were all sitting there look-
> ing at me . . . I wasn't impressed by the doctor's tone or atti-
> tude, he was on to me about taking out a barring order . . .
> the solicitor said it wasn't as simple as that, a lot of stuff
> was unproven . . . the solicitor was annoyed with the Health
> Board, he said they didn't know the legal profession . . . the
> doctor said if I didn't 'get a move on it' my daughter would
> be taken away, 'and you wouldn't like that, would you?' You
> were sitting there like a condemned woman . . . if the doctor
> put a question they would all look at you as if to say 'what's
> she going to say now?' . . . it was unbelievable . . .

The first mother had sensed discomfort at her presence:

> There was a bit of tension in the room when I went in there
> . . . I think they were afraid I'd blow their heads off or
> something . . .

With only one exception, all the parents whom we interviewed
expressed a preference for attending the whole case conference.
The one mother who expressed reservations about participating
felt that the professionals 'need to talk' and that while she would
like to hear what was being said, 'wouldn't know what to say . . .
don't think I'd like to be there'. Other parents, however, were
aware of potential discomfort but felt it would be worth it. One
said she would find it:

> . . . hard, upsetting and difficult, because they might have
> wanted to make decisions I didn't agree with . . . but I still
> would have liked to be there.

Another said:

> It would be hard and you do feel a bit vulnerable but you
> can't make an omelette without breaking eggs.

Others felt that their presence at the case conference could have
been valuable. The opportunities to meet everyone involved, and
to add some information, could have been used, 'it would help me
understand what it's about and what is good for the children'. Another mother said:

> I'd like to have known what was said about the family . . .
> could add something yourself as well. I wouldn't have been
> nervous . . . I don't know who was there anyway.

And another father greatly resented his life being discussed by a
group of professionals in his absence:

> It was all private . . . done behind my back . . . trying to
> take [his daughter] from me . . . there's all them people sit-
> ting around discussing my daughter . . . I would still prefer
> to go . . . better to go . . . I could defend myself.

The above findings illustrate strongly the dissatisfaction of parents with the level of participation in decision making afforded

them. Most of them expressed a wish to be more involved in the child protection process, and particularly to have the opportunity to attend case conferences about their families. The reaction of those parents who attended the end of meetings supports the research findings of Thoburn, Lewis and Shemmings (1995) and Farmer and Owen (1995) that 'partial' exclusion of parents tends to increase anxiety and distrust on their part. Other studies which replicate the findings here (Bell & Sinclair, 1993; Christie, 1993) also indicate that, although most parents were glad to attend case conferences, they often experienced them as painful and humiliating, highlighting the need to address this issue sensitively and to prepare all parties.

Parental Perceptions of Their Children's Current Situations

The majority of parents were satisfied with their children's progress since the child protection system became involved. One father described his twelve year old daughter as:

> . . . coming on bundles . . . she is very pleased with the counsellor, the sessions are being cut down now because she's making so much progress.

Other comments varied from 'great, much happier', 'fine in general', 'very happy' to 'brilliant'. Several commented on their children's school progress which they felt was a good indication of their welfare, and others mentioned that their children seemed to be getting better at making friends. Some reservations were expressed; one mother had recently found a suicide note in her daughter's room and was worried about her. Another was cautiously optimistic about her daughter's behaviour, saying 'she does actually seem to be improving . . . no complaints at the moment'. A father described his daughter as 'a little odd-going and distant . . . but healthy'. Another father was resigned to the possible re-emergence of problems:

> . . . she seems happy enough at home now . . . I hope anyway . . . but I don't know when she'll take off again . . . just have to take it one day at a time.

In one case, the children were in a foster home, and their mother was very satisfied with their care: 'they are all in good form, looked after well, dressed and clothed well . . . the foster parents are brilliant'.

Reservations were expressed in one situation, where the original social worker had left the area, and the family were no longer receiving any kind of service. The mother expressed concern about her daughter, who had been sexually abused. She felt the child still needed counselling:

> She's a typical teenager . . . but things have got to the stage when she can't talk about it anymore and we still don't talk about anything personal anymore . . . she should have stayed at counselling but she thought she wasn't getting any benefit . . . but as time goes by I can see she still needs it . . .

Parents' Perceptions of Their Own Situations

Although most of the children were deemed to be doing well and making progress, a significant number of the parents talked about feeling quite stressed themselves. While some felt they were getting on reasonably well, and appreciated the help they had been offered with the children, others were more resigned and perceived life as a kind of struggle: 'I've coped alone for long enough . . . will continue to do so', 'I'm shattered at what happened, but am now starting to look after myself'. A father said:

> The children are the main concern . . . I don't matter . . . I don't think there is any service that could help me . . . more money would be helpful and a chance to do a bit of socialising . . . the children are the main thing though . . .

Another lone father described his life:

> I'm depressed all the time . . . sometimes get suicidal . . . got a note from the psychiatrist but I tore it up . . . be afraid something I said would go against me . . .

The discovery of abuse and the process of the child abuse investigation had taken its toll on some parents, and left them very drained.

> I just go from day to day . . . it's when you have time to look back, that's the worst . . . I've become so unemotional after being through all that, and so depressed, they don't see me as doing anything really . . .

One mother, who was happy with the welfare of her children in foster care, expressed her own unhappiness:

> Very depressed and lonely . . . bored at home . . . miss the children. I find it hard to enjoy myself at all . . . I'm afraid in the house.

Another mother described herself as 'acutely distressed at times . . . worry about the children all the time'.

Despite the level of support that was being offered in relation to their children, parents did not generally perceive that the child protection system offered them any service for themselves. While most agreed that the priority of interventions should be the children involved, many commented on their own situation, and the fact that all the attention was directed towards the children. One woman, who had been extremely depressed around the time of the initial child abuse investigation, said:

> I had to go and talk to someone . . . there was no service for me. People are here for the girls and that's right, but there is nothing for me . . . I wasn't sleeping or eating . . . I felt suicidal . . .

A lone father suggested that:

> . . . there should be more opportunities to be given advice . . . the social workers are good . . . but there should be more supports . . . they have only offered a service to the twelve-year-old . . . there should be somewhere where you can let out your frustrations . . . how you feel every day . . . there are bound to be thousands of people in the same situation.

A mother whose daughter went into care for a while would have liked:

> . . . groups either in the hostel or somewhere else . . . to talk
> to others in the same situation . . . there was nothing like
> that available . . . or at least I was not told about it.

Some of the parents were also critical that the child protection investigation and ongoing involvement only concentrated on the children whose abuse had been discovered. The mother whose daughter came back into her custody after being abused by her father was worried about the other children living with him:

> I worry about the seventeen-year-old . . . the father doesn't
> give them any freedom . . . and the twelve-year-old because
> of the age she's coming to . . . her father is very rigid and
> picks and chooses her friends . . . she's going to be an ado-
> lescent soon . . . there is going to be trouble . . . I feel let
> down by the system.

Though a minority of parents we spoke to were in touch with members of their families, most of them said they had no support beyond what was offered by the child protection system, and were in many ways quite isolated. Money was a problem for most of them. The mother whose children were in foster care commented that:

> I couldn't give them what the foster parents do . . . if I had
> as much money as they had . . . no offence to them . . .

Two male lone parents felt that they were discriminated against, to some degree, as far as finances were concerned. One claimed that a social worker had confirmed this for him: 'She was straight – told me I'd "get nothing because you are a man"'; the other thought that he got less money than a female lone parent.

Some parents were critical of the way the concentration was focused on child protection, at the expense of wider family issues.

> No other problems were looked at at the time, like money or
> housing problems . . . I would definitely have been open to
> that . . . it doesn't just affect the victim, the whole family is
> affected by anything that is going on . . . my house is a

> hovel . . . I had just come out of so many years of abuse with
> this man . . . with the sexual abuse we had social workers,
> the Gardaí, the lot . . . the interviews . . . but when all that
> was done . . . full stop, that was it . . .

Another parent found that nobody was interested in his financial situation, which he found difficult to manage: 'I just have to get on with things myself'.

It appears, therefore, that, while parents appreciated the input from the child care services in relation to their children, some felt neglected, and found the focus on child protection to be narrow, and to exclude wider family concerns that they might have, such as worries about other children, and issues like poverty. They would have valued some counselling and practical services exclusively for themselves. Most of the parents we interviewed were isolated from their families and communities. The situations of some families were undoubtedly exacerbated by the circumstances surrounding the abuse incidents and their discovery, and at least four of the relationships had broken up because of sexual abuse and domestic violence.

Parental Views on Future Contact with the Child Protection Services

The majority of the parents we spoke to did not foresee that their contact with the social workers would end in the near future, except in one case where the girl involved was now an adult. A small number were unhappy about continued involvement.

> I wish they'd finish up . . . it's very embarrassing when I
> have a friend in and a social worker comes knocking on the
> door.

Another parent was resigned:

> It will keep dragging on I suppose . . . they've been coming
> for a long time . . . I don't know how long they will be com-
> ing for . . . it's not up to me I suppose . . .

One mother who hadn't seen a social worker since the last one had left indicated that she was now ready for contact:

> I'd probably value contact with a social worker now because things are going so badly at home. I didn't want it at the time, but you get very overwhelmed . . . so many interviews going on . . . never even thought ahead . . . they could have been a bit pushier . . . people going through that are not in a frame of mind to think of what's going on in the next couple of months or anything . . .

Other parents were happy for contact with the child care services to continue, and some were very keen to keep it going: 'I hope they don't stop now', 'they were actually going to close the case a couple of weeks ago . . . I wouldn't like that to happen'. However, the lack of any notion on the parents' part of where their work with the Health Board was heading, or what mutual aims they shared with the child protection services, once again indicates a need for shared plans and agreements.

CONCLUSION

The concept of parental partnership is gaining increasing importance in child protection policy, and research has highlighted its importance in terms of positive outcomes. Social workers who were interviewed expressed some difficulty in maintaining democratic relationships with families where there was hostility and non-co-operation. They perceived their own powerful positions *vis-à-vis* the families as determining a false level of partnership at times, where families were left with little choice.

Over three-quarters of the parents involved in the sample cases accepted our invitation to participate in the study. Where parents were not suspected themselves of perpetuating the concern that led to investigations, their experience of the child protection system was tolerable, and in some cases quite positive. However, where they were suspected of abusing their children, they found the system quite harsh and stigmatising, and were very fearful that their children would be taken into care. Though some parents found the Gardaí helpful, many of them were unhappy about their involvement in the investigations, depicting them as insensitive, uncommunicative, inclined to make false promises and disinterested in domestic violence. Several parents suggested that specialist police should be appointed to child protection work.

Mothers whose children were abused by ex-husbands or partners acknowledged the danger that had been present, but a significant number of parents still perceived the risk to their children at the time of investigation to have been minimal and not perpetrated by themselves. Despite this, the majority of parents had engaged well with the child protection services, and valued them. Assessment, therapeutic and family support work was rated highly by parents, and direct work with children was also particularly valued. Deficits were pointed out, where services had ground to a halt, or personnel had left and delays in replacement were experienced. In some instances, parents complained about lack of trust and openness from the workers, and felt that information was kept from them.

Parents seemed aware of the discomfort that full participation at case conferences could cause them, but nonetheless expressed a strong desire to attend them, and cited the advantages for them of full attendance at such meetings. Most parents reported positively on their children's progress and attributed this, in the main, to the involvement of the child protection system. However, they clearly identified a shortage of services specifically for themselves, and in some cases felt that there was an over-concentration on their children's safety, with little concern about their own situations. A significant number of parents were highly stressed, and some were suffering from depression. Their adversities were compounded by the fact that many of the parents were isolated from their families, some having separated from partners because of the abuse incident. In addition to this, the majority of them had financial problems, and were experiencing problems with their other children who had not been the focus of investigation or assessment.

Findings from both phases of this study suggest that, to a great extent, parents were not involved in a meaningful way with the child protection system, particularly in the early, investigative stages. This deficit was further highlighted by the way in which parents themselves expressed the wish for greater participation. In our view, this strongly highlights the need for the situation to

be considered and some measures taken to redress the power imbalance and to work towards the possibility of productive and
meaningful participation of families in the child protection process.

The next chapter moves away from the process and content of
child protection in the sample cases, to a broader perspective on
the child protection system in general, and reflects the views of all
the professionals whom we interviewed.

Chapter Seven

The Child Protection System

Introduction

The delivery of a child protection service depends on a number of variables within the system, and can be helped or hindered to a degree by the way in which these operate. The findings discussed in this chapter emerged from the comments made by various professionals, not all in response to direct questions, but used to illustrate different points made in relation to the cases under study. We felt they were both valuable and insightful, and needed to be included.

Co-ordination of Work between Different Disciplines

The aspect of practice which provoked most comment from the professionals whom we interviewed concerned co-ordination of work between different disciplines and the fostering of good working relationships. It was felt that current efforts at co-operative working needed to be maintained and strengthened, due to the complex and multi-faceted nature of the work. One Garda stressed the need to combine approaches:

> It's sad that with all the agencies, bad cases still happen. It's difficult in the home situation . . . hard to break the seal . . . it underlines the need to work together.

It was generally acknowledged that inter-agency and inter-professional relationships in child protection work had improved over the past few years. A medical social worker spoke of the importance of 'new links forged with other hospital professionals', and another social worker was positive about meetings with the Gardaí, which she described as 'helpful . . . though more work needs to be done there'. It was also felt that the case conference, another forum for co-ordinated work, had improved in quality. However, despite the improvement in working relationships, there were still misgivings about the willingness of professionals to share responsibility as well as tasks. Professionals inside and outside the Health Board had a lot to say on this and were all wary of being isolated in their dealings with risky situations. A teacher felt strongly about it:

> School is left to monitor very serious cases . . . there is a need for more sharing of responsibility and co-operation between different professionals . . . we need back-up from psychologists; teachers can't do everything.

And a public health nurse suggested that:

> . . . there should be more sharing of responsibility and working together, especially between public health nurses and social workers.

However, social workers, both inside and outside the Health Board, and in both Community Care and psychiatric settings, felt very strongly that they should not have to bear the full burden. A social worker from a community child psychiatric service commented:

> . . . the notion of shared responsibility for child protection and working together . . . of child protection not being the concern of the Health Board only, needs to be addressed . . . as while relations are a lot better than before and other professionals do refer [cases], the ultimate responsibility lies with the social worker and the rest generally carry out a minimal role.

This appears to be a particular problem for Community Care social workers, who commented that sometimes they are so caught up with investigating new cases, that their input into already open cases is curtailed. The input of other key professionals into the open cases could, they felt, sometimes be sufficient, but 'social workers tend to retain responsibility for them if anything goes wrong' and they resent the notion of having to do this. One social worker commented that:

> Social workers should not be the only professionals involved
> in child protection . . . responsibility should be shared with
> other professionals.

Ironically, despite the social workers' convictions, it does seem
that other professionals would like to be recognised as having a
more responsible role. Teachers in particular felt that the importance of their contributions was not acknowledged:

> The school is not taken sufficient account of within the sys-
> tem . . . for example in the Kilkenny incest inquiry report
> there is one paragraph in the whole report about the case
> . . . there is a total lack of awareness of what goes on in the
> school . . .

Another teacher from a different area made a similar point:
'teachers know so much, they should be an essential part of any
team in an area' and advocated the setting up of a committee:

> . . . at least one representative from each school on a local
> committee or team, where you would have a psychologist, a
> Garda, a social worker, a general practitioner . . .

Likewise, residential child care workers felt that they did important work that was not always given due acknowledgement:

> . . . the child care worker should be given more credit and
> recognition . . . the Health Board child care workers get a
> better deal . . . they are given more scope, responsibility and
> recognition . . . this should happen in residential child care
> also . . .

And another residential child care worker from a different Community Care area held a similar view:

> Ours is a very important role . . . the reason children are in
> care is because they are from a dysfunctional family back-
> ground . . . if the child is returning home you have to ensure
> that the place is a safe environment . . . we supervise home
> visits, and have to ensure that they are safe . . . it is our re-
> sponsibility, so it needs to be better recognised.

Organisational Issues

The increase in social work and child care posts in the South Eastern Health Board, while welcome, has, in combination with high turnover of practitioners, created its own problems. A teacher lamented the lack of continuity of workers:

> It's better to deal with the same person. I don't know why there is so much movement in social services . . . there is nobody in this particular area, it's 'piggy in the middle' . . . I would like to see them linked in more in the area, and left in the area for longer.

The extra numbers resulted in an increasing need for supervision. A social worker commented that 'the increase in staff without increase of support for staff' contributed to the 'vicious circle' of high turnover: 'there have been a lot of temporary staff . . . the work is stressful and they are not staying'. The changes have other implications too:

> . . . the large team means less camaraderie and closeness . . . this is essential to team work, so the system needs to address this.

Social workers in particular felt that the issue of caseload management needed to be addressed. This would involve increasing supervision, reducing caseloads, and most importantly, improvements in planning. There was a definite sense, expressed by one practitioner, that 'social workers are overloaded with responsibility with not enough support'. There appeared to be the need to address what one worker described as 'a sense of chaos in my own work which I feel is the same with others . . . no time to plan, take stock of what is going on'. The need to ensure time was available to 'plan team priorities' and 'look at the overall system' was emphasised, as was the need to diversify methods of working:

> . . . there needs to be a greater awareness of high risk categories of families . . . particular approaches need to be taken to the various categories . . . not to be treating all child care concerns as if they can all be dealt with by a similar response.

Social workers believed that the need to constantly respond to new child abuse referrals left them very little time to get an overall sense of the direction their work was taking, and they wanted to try and deal with this.

> There's a need for a more formal process of evaluating and reviewing cases in depth as opposed to dealing with the day to day progress of the case.

> There should be a way of allowing time – looking at caseloads on a team rather than an individual basis, time to reflect is important and unless it is specifically given it won't be available.

Practitioners suggested more extensive use of planning days and team meetings, both for doing this work, and for considering their broader professional orientations:

> Work has changed a lot, and there is a need to think about that, and discuss it, and see where it is going and what the role of the social worker is.

On a more practical note, they advocated the introduction of a case weighting system, rather than the current policy of allocating cases according to 'the patch'.

Training

The appointment of a training officer to the region was generally welcomed by the Health Board employees we interviewed, though they suggested that the level and type of training still needed development: 'the training officer is too spread around'. There was strong support for an increase in 'in-service' training on 'various aspects of social work' and 'study days, study groups for team building and for ongoing training and learning'. Social workers in particular highlighted the need for 'regular training in child protection to be prioritised' and 'more specific child protection training'. The need for induction training was also pointed out. A new social worker, who had recently trained, indicated that while the child abuse procedures were very useful for new staff, they were not enough, even in combination with professional qualifications.

> There are no clear directives [in the guidelines] as to who
> should do what and how an interview should be conducted.
> Six months of child protection training doesn't give experi-
> ence or skills.

And another worker felt she would have usefully gained from
some initial induction:

> . . . should have had time when I started for getting familiar
> with the services, need to know what the services are . . .
> instead I was plugged straight into work.

'Easier access to training opportunities' for basic grade workers
was also requested, rather than the current practice where
training seemed to be mostly reserved for staff in management
positions. Equally, there was strong interest and recognition of the
need for multi-disciplinary seminars and workshops which would
include a broad range of professionals, from inside and outside the
Board.

Working Conditions

Accommodation in some social work offices was very problematic,
and unsatisfactory. In one of the areas, all the social workers
shared one office and three telephones. The noise level was very
high in the main office, which obviously impaired individual
workers' ability to concentrate on their work, and afforded them
no privacy to write up their case-notes. There was one interview
room in this area, described by one of the social workers as 'not
conducive to confidentiality, for someone going to discuss child
sexual abuse it is not conducive . . . the atmosphere is very cold'.
In fact, interview space was very limited in all areas, which meant
that social workers had to continually vacate their offices to provide space where clients could be seen, thus disrupting their
work. In another Community Care area, two social workers
shared a room which had only one telephone. The room was also
used for a psychiatric clinic once a month.

   Administrative/clerical back up for the child protection workers was poor in most areas. In one centre, one staff member was
typing and doing administrative work for fourteen to twenty
workers, resulting in a back-log. Most of the health centres had

only one clerical officer to do the receptionist and secretarial work for all the personnel based there, which meant that individual workers had very little access to her time. At the time of the study, the allocation of administrative staff to case conferences was inconsistent, and often minutes were not written up for some time afterwards.

Personal Safety

Child protection work can be frightening at times, carried out, as it often is, in an atmosphere of tension and heightened emotions. Sixteen out of the eighteen social workers interviewed had experienced physical or verbal threats to their personal safety at some point in their recent careers. As one social worker pointed out, this issue did not constantly pre-occupy them, but that was most likely 'because of naiveté more than anything . . . we don't think of the risks . . .' Rural visiting was identified as a potentially dangerous practice when practitioners were working late in the evening, particularly in the winter time, in isolated areas.

When asked if there were any supports to assist social workers in dealing with this threat to their personal safety, one social worker expressed a vague knowledge about a 'safety officer' in the Health Board, but did not know exactly who this was or what their role was. Otherwise, no formal structure for support was identified by the social workers interviewed. The one common informal support identified by the social workers was joint visiting with either a Senior/Team Leader or a colleague. All respondents said they would have no difficulty asking a colleague or senior to accompany them and that this practice was supported and encouraged. However, some workers claimed that they were reluctant to ask their busy managers to accompany them as often as they considered necessary. Another worker pointed out that, while she favoured joint visiting, she frequently works in isolation and does not have a colleague nearby whom she can ask.

Other workers have asked Gardaí to accompany them on visits where they feared aggression, and found them very willing to assist them, though not always free to do so. One worker had availed of the opportunity to see a potentially abusive client in the local Garda station. Some social workers had built in their own 'security' systems which included asking to see a client in the office rather than at home if the worker is fearful of his/her aggression, requesting colleagues to check in to the office every ten to fifteen minutes.

As well as acknowledging the value of the informal supports, all respondents made suggestions for improving the protection of staff in relation to both home visiting and working in the office. These include: easy access to a phone, access to a health centre or office within a reasonable distance of the location being visited, or possession of a mobile phone. In fact, one social worker had considered buying a mobile phone herself due to the level of vulnerability she felt when visiting clients in rural areas. A number of practitioners suggested the carrying of personal alarms/bleepers linked up to a central system. Dog alarms were also considered essential by some. One worker made the useful suggestion that a structure for recording the location of workers at any one time in all health centres should operate consistently: a 'where are you book' in which practitioners could record their itinerary and expected return time, particularly necessary in areas where a social worker could be out of the office all day. A formal back-up service to support home visiting was also suggested, rather than the *ad hoc* system that currently operated.

A number of practitioners also identified general safety issues in the buildings where they were normally based, some reporting that the centres they work in have no porters or receptionists, and that clients could walk straight into their rooms. Many recommended the installation of buzzers, but recognised that they would be useless in the absence of other colleagues.

The need for training in personal safety was identified. A number of workers acknowledged that they and their colleagues take too many risks and fail to take necessary protective precautions when home visiting.

CHILD ABUSE PROCEDURES AND GUIDELINES

The South Eastern Health Board introduced their child abuse procedures in 1993. These, together with the *Department of Health Child Abuse Guidelines*, and the 1995 guidelines for the *Notification of Suspected Cases of Child Abuse between the Health*

Boards and the Gardaí, formed the basis of the child protection system in operation at the time of this study. We included some discussion on these in our interviews, to see if practitioners were actually conversant with them, and they found them effective as a framework.

Social workers had a good knowledge of the Department of Health guidelines, though two of them had not read the regional procedures, one worker having been away when they were introduced, and the other one having only started the job recently. With some exceptions, most of the non social work professionals whom we interviewed said they were familiar with the *Department of Health Child Abuse Guidelines*. Those who were not included a school counsellor, a home help, a psychologist, a Garda sergeant, and a teacher. The Gardaí were aware of their own profession's procedures and the teacher reported that while she wasn't familiar with the Department of Education's own child abuse guidelines she would talk to her principal if she had any concerns. With the exception of two teachers and a home help, and a different Garda, the majority of practitioners also knew the regional procedures.

While there were mixed views on the quality of child abuse guidelines in general, most social workers found them useful, and thought they had an important role. Comments on their efficacy included: 'the guidelines are good, in that it sets stuff out', 'working reasonably well – especially the notification system', 'you are clear what you are doing, which is difficult in child protection work' and 'really helpful'.

Other professionals also found them useful. A County Council social worker described them as 'an improvement . . . an important guide for practice' and a psychologist said 'it means we are taking child abuse seriously'. A child care worker suggested that they:

> . . . give a framework, help to point out the issues . . . with them you know something will happen, a case will not be just left . . . yes, I think they are very important.

And another child care worker considered standardisation very important:

It means that people are doing more or less the same thing
. . . set patterns should emerge . . . you can't really go wrong
. . . good to help own work and that of others, good to be
backed up by procedures . . . if an issue arises you can go
back to them and check things out.

Some practitioners were more qualified in their praise of the child
abuse guidelines. One Garda emphasised the need to be realistic
about them: 'Of course everything doesn't happen like a textbook'
and one social worker suggested that they had:

. . . gone down with the folklore . . . I mean I'm not sure how
closely they are followed . . . they tend to get watered down
with practice.

A child guidance social worker also had reservations about the
utility of enforcing guidelines without flexibility:

The role regarding the procedures is not always so clear cut
. . . there's a need for active liaison rather than rigid interpretation of roles.

Professionals who worked with young people felt that following
child abuse guidelines could create dilemmas, particularly where
older children were concerned:

When working with teenagers, the issue of reporting to the
Gardaí and the Health Board can be difficult, as older teenagers in particular may not want this to happen, especially
if the abuse is retrospective . . . raises confidentiality and
ethical issues . . . the responsibility to inform parents of allegations and details is not so clear cut when working with
older teenagers.

A school counsellor had a similar view:

I think that clients should have the choice of when to report
and also they should be able to say if they do not want to
press charges and just get counselling . . . children should
have some power here . . . it's a difficult area . . . there are
parents' rights and children's rights and they have to be
balanced and looked after . . . you have to protect all involved . . . but some rules in the system are to the detriment

of the child . . . or where the child does not want the Health Board or parents told . . . what do we do? . . . if we go to the Health Board, it automatically becomes official – so how do you look after both parents' and child's interest in this regard?

Once again, the perception of child protection as the social workers' responsibility was seen to be reflected in the way procedures were used. Social workers from Community Care felt that other practitioners were reluctant to play their part:

> There is the attitude that it is really 'social work procedures' as opposed to for *all* professionals . . . other professionals tend to refer cases to the social worker for them to notify, or will merely fill out the form, send it in and make no attempt to follow up or liaise . . . sometimes a public health nurse or a teacher will guarantee confidentiality when this can't be followed through on . . .

However, a public health nurse was quite clear that she had a responsibility to make a notification if the need arose:

> I think it's appropriate for public health nurses to do this if they are the ones who have made the referral . . . I don't mind doing the preliminary reports . . . I'm happy enough overall with this.

But another public health nurse felt that her colleagues were uncomfortable with the notification process, including writing the preliminary reports.

> There needs to be clarification about what the preliminary report should contain, and the public health nurses should not be afraid of the preliminary report . . . they are a bit nervous of writing these reports and need to know that they will be supported.

Teachers appeared to have some discomfort with the notion of being identified with notifying allegations. According to one:

> A lot of teachers are not comfortable with being named . . . social workers and Gardaí can say who they are [the teachers]. If teachers are not named, they would be freer to re-

port to their principal if they didn't have this hanging over
them . . .

Some practitioners were concerned about the 'narrowing' effect of
procedures, which tended to focus very much on investigation, at
the cost of longer term work.

> Guidelines can be very bald . . . all the guidelines want to
> do is to push it out . . . get the duty done . . . report the case
> . . . fill in the forms . . . but this should only be a small part
> of the whole process . . . guidelines don't take account of the
> role of the school or take the school into consideration . . .
> nor do they look at the long term management of cases.

A Community Care social worker also felt 'there is a risk of losing
the human aspect by focusing too much on procedures'. A school
counsellor expressed the view that some flexibility was needed in
the use of guidelines:

> At the moment if you report something to the Health Board
> it automatically becomes official . . . there is no room for in-
> formal negotiation first . . . there should be a waiting period
> where you can have informal contact with the Health Board
> without them going *gung ho* for the procedures . . . a hold-
> ing time, say a week or two . . .

Suggestions for modifications in the guidelines were offered.
Teachers reiterated their reluctance to be named and suggested
that there should be:

> . . . anonymity for teachers. Teachers don't want to be fin-
> gered. There could be dreadful repercussions if you reported
> a child . . . it's open to abuse. Things get insinuated . . .

A child guidance social worker suggested 'more flexibility about
notifying Gardaí of retrospective abuse . . . should be time limits'
and a child care worker felt that her own profession merited more
recognition in them: '. . . a separate section on the child care
worker's role in investigation and management of child abuse'. It
was also suggested that procedures should be more oriented towards the realities and complexities of cases, and tapered towards

individual situations. The need for consensus on both their construction and operation was stressed:

> There is a need for clear guidelines about all cases and time should be made available to discuss them, without just bringing them in.

Social workers were keen to enlist the co-operation of other colleagues in the child protection network, and felt the guidelines should address that:

> Other professionals need to be made more clear of their responsibility in relation to the procedures and their responsibility to follow through on cases they have notified . . . there needs to be generally more understanding of other professionals and of the nature of child protection . . . for example, that you can't guarantee confidentiality . . .

Another social worker, from a different area, also aspired towards more sharing of responsibility:

> Other professionals need to be more actively involved in the procedures and responsibility . . . procedures at present imply that social workers are the only ones with responsibility for [dealing with] child abuse.

A key topic of discussion in relation to procedures and guidelines was the issue of mandatory reporting, which was quite topical at the time the fieldwork was carried out. We asked a number of professionals from outside Community Care for their views on this. In general, the responses were guarded and conditional. While no professionals appeared to strongly oppose mandatory reporting, many identified potential difficulties associated with its introduction. Social workers outside the Health Board were concerned that it might have an inhibiting effect because of the 'fear of litigation and of issues being driven back underground':

> On the one hand it's a good idea, but it may stop people from referring at all if they can't remain anonymous . . . or if a teacher or neighbour has a hunch but is not sure, now they can't ring and discuss the case, without making a false report . . . it may stop people doing this . . . Mandatory re-

porting may increase referrals initially but they are likely
to decrease in the long run as people will stop talking or
telling anyone, such as teachers, about concerns or allegations . . . it's important not to put teachers in a position
where trust could be jeopardised.

A public health nurse also wondered if mandatory reporting
might inhibit referrers:

You need to be careful not to accuse someone in the wrong .
. . people are getting more wary of reporting and if mandatory reporting comes in, this will be even more . . . there
will be more and more anonymous calls which you can do
nothing about.

The potential for breached trust and damage to therapeutic relationships was brought up by a psychologist:

It's a good idea in general, but you have to be careful . . . in
therapy children can often be very nervous giving details
and I think if I had to report everything, this might prevent
them even more . . . you need to be careful and consider
when is an appropriate time to report, in what circumstances and what will the consequences for the child be . . .

And a child care worker was also concerned about the child's position:

There can be benefits I know, but you have to take the
child's wishes into account . . . the trauma for the child . . .
the decision to report should be discussed with the child . . .
especially if you are talking about teenagers . . . and also
you have to take account of the repercussions for the child .
. . the outcome . . . it's very hard, the child still loves the
family and is fearful of isolation and rejection . . . I don't
know how this can be taken into account in mandatory reporting.

The importance of legal immunity was stressed by another child
care worker:

If you have a suspicion you should always refer it . . . but
there has to be a system where there is no fear of recrimi-

nation . . . there needs to be a privilege, like in the Dáil,
that the person reporting cannot be sued.

It appears that, while there was a certain amount of support for
the notion of mandatory reporting, there was no certainty or
agreement that its introduction would be either operable or beneficial for children. A teacher sounded a further word of caution: 'I
hope people don't think that mandatory reporting means that
problems will go away'.

THE DIRECTION OF THE CHILD PROTECTION SYSTEM

One of the key points which emerged from this study was the
strong concern voiced by practitioners about the way in which
concerns about children and families were, more and more, being
framed in terms of identification and investigation of child abuse,
at the expense of a broader, welfare orientation.

Thorpe (1994), and Gibbons, Conroy and Bell (1995) commented, on the basis of their research, that the 'narrowing' of
child abuse definitions has meant that only child sexual abuse
and incidents which have a 'visible' impact, such as injuries or
bruising, are considered worthy of a response. These views were
replicated by some practitioners we interviewed, who were concerned particularly about the dominant profile of child sexual
abuse, which one social worker felt was compounded by the setting up of the child sexual abuse assessment service. 'Child sexual
abuse has always taken over, but the setting up of the unit has
meant that it has really taken over now'. A psychologist believed
that:

> At the moment, it's as if child sexual abuse is more impor-
> tant than any other kind of abuse . . . the area of emotional
> abuse is still not being recognised as serious . . . I always
> report it, but I feel it has not been clearly defined yet, and
> it's not clear how to act on it.

Social workers, even more than other professionals, were con-
scious of the increasingly forensic direction their work was taking.

> I'm worried about the emphasis on investigation . . . we are
> working like detectives at the expense of following up work.

Another social worker was becoming increasingly disillusioned
with this:

> The nature of social work is changing . . . becoming more of
> a police force . . . if I was choosing a career option again, I
> couldn't choose social work as it is presently. Protection has
> become foremost and prevention/support is only secondary
> and not happening enough . . .

The focus on risk assessment and the fact that the work was 'too
child protection oriented' meant, according to a number of professionals that there was 'not enough emphasis on prevention and
treatment'. A social worker pointed out that:

> The social work role should be less to police the family and
> more to enable families . . . they need the resources to take
> a more preventive focus.

A public health nurse was critical that:

> . . . the system is very insufficient from the point of view of
> prevention . . . you couldn't say at the moment there is any
> sort of preventive programme going on . . . it is merely crisis
> . . . the situation is worsening . . . there are similar levels of
> child abuse here as in the cities even though many do not
> think so . . . it's harder to address because of the secrecy of
> the country.

And a local authority social worker agreed with her:

> The present system is mostly reactionary and there is a
> need for a more preventative supportive approach . . . I'm
> afraid it's getting more and more narrowly defined, centred
> around fixed guidelines and procedures.

Professionals acknowledged that it was very difficult not to focus
their work towards investigation. A social worker commented that
'there is a feeling of constantly watching your back'. A community
psychiatric nurse highlighted the paradoxical nature of child protection:

> It's a tricky area . . . there is the problem of, if you inter-
> vene too soon, you are criticised and yet, if you leave things,
> you are criticised.

And one child care worker warned about the dangers of being
over-cautious:

> It's wrong to pick out one case and equal every other case to
> it . . . that is what happened with the Kilkenny Inquiry . . .
> you shouldn't try to generalise this to the system . . . I think
> the social workers, nurses and so on do their jobs as well as
> they can . . .

Several professionals considered that the image of social work as
a 'helping' profession was suffering due to its association with investigation. A school counsellor felt that this should be addressed:

> The image of social workers has to change . . . it needs to be
> improved . . . at the moment, referring a family to the social
> worker is the worst thing imaginable . . . parents and chil-
> dren see social workers presently as interfering busybodies
> . . . so you need to put a humane face on social workers . . .
> make parents less afraid. Maybe the legal side of social
> work needs to be separated, maybe the Gardaí could do this
> and leave the social worker to the counselling or supportive
> role . . . or else delay the procedures and legal intervention.

And a home help was concerned that mothers might be reluctant
to approach the child care services in case it reflected badly on
themselves:

> There needs to be information available to mothers and
> children that there is help, and to have no fears about being
> reprimanded if they go to look for help.

The need for sensitivity in child care work was emphasised. A
teacher pointed to the need for child centredness:

> It's a difficult area, there are parents' rights and children's
> rights and they have to be balanced and looked after . . .
> you have to protect all involved . . . but some rules in the
> system are to the detriment of the child.

And one Garda reinforced the priority of children's needs:

> A child should be at home first and foremost. You can't go
> overboard . . . you have to try and work within the home,
> and pulling a child out should be the last resort.

Professionals were also concerned about high public expectations
that a well resourced child protection system will mean the eradi-
cation of child abuse. A child care worker, referring to the *Report
of the Kilkenny Incest Investigation*, said:

> I don't think that we will ever be able to prevent cases like
> this happening . . . with hindsight it is easy to judge.

And there was a similar reflection from a community psychiatric
nurse:

> I don't think anything the services do will prevent certain
> cases of abuse from happening . . . the system is as good as
> it can be . . . it is doing as much as it can I think.

A family therapist commented on the unreal assumption that professionals can achieve the impossible:

> It's unrealistic to think you can protect against all child
> abuse, no matter what kind of a system you have . . . how
> can you move into a family that don't want you?

CONCLUSION

This chapter has reflected the views of a range of professionals on
the child protection system. In particular, it has focused on various aspects of service delivery, the usefulness of procedures and
guidelines, and, in a general sense, the direction of the child protection system.

Inter-agency and inter-professional co-ordination appear to
have improved in the region in recent years, though social workers signified their discomfort at having to bear what they considered to be an unfair burden of responsibility for child protection.
Social workers in particular expressed a sense of 'chaos' around
some of their work, due to what they perceived as pressure on
them to carry out so many child abuse investigations. At an or-

ganisational level, problems were identified in relation to the high staff turnover that has resulted from an expansion in the service, and in the pressure put on the services by the recent increase in referrals. The need for more support in terms of supervision and caseload management generally was recognised, and a desire to have recent training initiatives extended was expressed, in particular those of a multi-disciplinary nature. The inadequacy of office accommodation was highlighted, along with the shortage of clerical support in many of the centres where staff were based. Because of this, most practitioners felt they were poorly facilitated to carry out their work to the required standard. The issue of personal safety was raised, and a number of suggestions were offered by social workers for a stepping up of security arrangements to protect them in vulnerable situations.

We found that most practitioners were familiar with the procedures which were directly relevant to their own profession, though a number of those outside the Health Board indicated their lack of familiarity with the national guidelines. Reservations were expressed about the limiting nature of procedures and the majority of practitioners had doubts about the wisdom of implementing mandatory reporting of suspected child abuse.

Discomfort with the forensic emphasis on child protection work was expressed, and the shortage of time available to do preventive work was lamented. Finally, serious concern was expressed about the public perception of the service. While practitioners had a positive view of their contributions towards the protection of children, they felt the public at large, and professionals outside their immediate network, had unrealistic and over-optimistic expectations of their ability to address the very complex issues which arise in cases of child abuse and neglect.

CHAPTER EIGHT

CONCLUSION

As outlined in Chapter One, the overall aim of the research was to examine the nature of child protection practices in one health board area in Ireland. We began with a brief historical overview of the development of child welfare services in Ireland and discussed a number of issues that have resulted in the substantial changes which are currently occurring in the Irish child welfare system. We followed this with a discussion of recent research in the United Kingdom and Ireland pertinent to the research. The research itself began with an examination of the way in which general referrals to the service were responded to, in comparison to alleged child abuse and neglect referrals. Following on from this, an in-depth analysis of the initial and ongoing management of cases which were notified as suspected child abuse and neglect in May-June 1995 was carried out. This was examined in Phase One by analysing all of the notifications made during the two month period and, in Phase Two, through an analysis of eighteen of those cases in even greater depth. The main areas examined within this context were:

- the role of social workers in the child welfare system;

- the nature of inter-agency and inter-professional co-operation;

- the effectiveness of case conferences;

- the perspective of parents and their level of participation in the process and, interviewees' perceptions of the overall system of child protection within the health board.

In this final chapter, we aim to discuss the key findings of the research and examine them in relation to similar research undertaken elsewhere. We do this with the aim of highlighting the complexities and ambiguities in child welfare apparatuses, the ideologies that construct the intervention of various agencies, and the factors likely to shape the child welfare apparatus in the future.

OVERVIEW OF RESEARCH FINDINGS

The social work service of the South Eastern Health Board area was found to be primarily a child protection and welfare service. While there is much evidence of prioritising of child abuse and neglect within health boards from the 1980s onwards, our research showed that persons referred for more general problems shared similar socio-economic circumstances with those referred to the service for child abuse and neglect concerns. Furthermore, both categories examined appeared to share similar family difficulties which were either one of the reasons for referral or were identified as problems present at the time of referral. The only significant difference between the two categories was that cases referred in relation to child abuse and neglect allegations appeared to be experiencing a greater number of other family difficulties, in addition to the child abuse concern. However, this finding may be as much due to the fact that such cases received greater attention and thus more in-depth assessments were possible which allowed for identification of the broad range of difficulties those families were experiencing. The fact that many of the general referrals were seen on a once-off basis suggests that collection of such detailed information was not possible to attain nor thought relevant at the time. Throughout the research, this primary focus on child protection and welfare became apparent. For example, social workers were found to be more likely to define progress in their work in terms of the child abuse issue rather than progress for the family in more general terms and when progress was considered in this broader sphere, it was found to be less positive. This suggests that the service is framed primarily to respond to child abuse and neglect, offering limited resources or energy for addressing broader family needs, even with the families with whom they were actively involved. The main reasons for this appear to be the increasing national concern relating to child abuse (emanating primarily from a number of recent child abuse inquiries within health boards, including the South Eastern

Board), and the huge increase in the numbers of referrals of suspected child abuse and neglect to the health boards over the past five years in particular. While extra resources have been made available following the implementation of the *Child Care Act, 1991*, it seems that the demands on the child protection element of the social work service have limited provision of supportive and preventative resources to families where children are at risk.

PROCEDURES AND DISCRETION

Procedures and guidelines were found to be of great significance, particularly at the initial stages of intervention, where they ultimately framed the response of the social work service. Social workers were the key personnel who appeared to carry responsibility for implementing procedures, such as informing the Director of Community Care of the alleged abuse, informing the Gardaí of suspected child abuse or neglect, seeing the parents and children following the allegations. The social work service was also found to be primarily responsible for co-ordinating the involvement of other professionals or agencies in part or all of the initial investigation process. Social workers generally implemented the recommended procedures in response to allegations, but often did so in a discretionary manner. For example, in Phase One of the research, it was shown that a number of notifications to the Director of Community Care were not made within the recommended time frame. While the reasons for the delay in notifying were not specifically examined, it would appear that social workers tended to use their discretion in relation to the guidelines, waiting to gain further information or to check out details before submitting a formal notification. A similar process seems to have occurred in relation to notification of the Garda. In some instances, social workers deemed it more appropriate to initially make *informal* contact with the Gardaí, rather than going through the *formal* procedures. Social workers themselves recognised the importance of clear guidelines for child protection practice, but were also wary of procedures and guidelines becoming 'procedure for procedure sake'.

ROLES OF RESPONSIBILITY IN CHILD PROTECTION WORK

As outlined earlier, at both the initial and ongoing stages of case management, social workers were found to be the front line workers in the system. Even where social workers had limited contact with families, or where other professionals were more involved, the social worker was almost always identified as the person carrying the key responsibility for the main protection role. It is interesting that, on the one hand, social workers were critical of the concentration of this responsibility on themselves alone, yet, on the other hand, a number of other professionals expressed a frustration with not being sufficiently involved, nor being given responsibility within the system.

While social workers operated most frequently as the front-line personnel over the process of intervention with alleged child abuse and neglect cases, the role of other professionals both within the Health Board and outside of it was hugely significant throughout. Phase One findings highlight, for example, the crucial role other professionals played in the initial identification and referral of alleged abuse or neglect to the service. It was generic services such as teachers and school principles, public health nurses and GPs who most frequently made such referrals to the service. The same professionals were also most likely to have been involved with the families referred, in relation to particular individual or family difficulties, prior to, and following, initial social work involvement. Other more specialist professionals, such as psychologists, social workers from other agencies, child care workers and hospital staff, were involved in a number of the cases examined in both Phase One and Two, at some stage of the intervention. The findings in this research illuminate the considerable role played by professionals, other than community care social workers, at each stage of the child protection process.

PROFESSIONAL COLLABORATION

On the whole, good working relations existed between social workers and other professionals. The most beneficial aspect of such relations were identified by both the social workers and the other professionals as being the ability to pool resources of the different professionals, being able to facilitate one another and provide mutual support in intervention with families. However, some areas were identified which could limit effective inter-agency and inter-professional co-operation. The most significant of these were the frustrations of long waiting lists in some services, the slowness of the legal system in taking action, inadequate communication and feedback on particular cases, and frequent turnover of staff.[1] The professional relationships which were found to be most in need of addressing were those between social workers and the Gardaí. While positive relations were reported in some instances, the need for closer working relations, better communication, improved sharing of information and the development of a better understanding of each other's roles was emphasised by both Gardaí and social workers. Both sets of professionals expected that some of these difficulties would be addressed with the full implementation of the *Guidelines for Notification of Suspected Child Abuse Between the Health Boards and the Gardaí* (1995) and the continuation of the joint training initiative between Gardaí and social workers, which was in place during the time of the study.

A principle feature of inter-agency and inter-professional co-operation was the centrality of informal communication and relations in enhancing good working relations. Such informal networks have proved to be hugely important, especially in the context of a primarily rural based social work service. However, while recommending that such personal and informal relations be encouraged and supported, the need for more formal lines of communication and co-operation was also considered crucial to ensure an effective and sustainable child protection system.

CASE CONFERENCES

The one formal mechanism which did exist to facilitate inter-agency and inter-professional co-operation was the use of case conferences. Most social workers and other professionals found the case conference process to be a valuable and useful mecha-

---

[1] The issue of turnover of staff was related directly to the Community Care social work professionals, whereas the other limitations were identified by both social workers and other professionals as key concerns.

nism for facilitating effective intervention, at both the initial and ongoing stages of involvement with families. The main advantages of the case conferences were identified as their usefulness in facilitating the sharing of information, making joint working plans, sharing responsibility and allocating tasks. However, some reservations were also expressed, particularly about the time-consuming nature of the case conferences. The process was sometimes found by various professionals to be dominated by reporting and discussion, leaving little time for decision making. Some social workers were critical of the unrealistic nature of some case conference recommendations and the fact that it was most often the social worker who was left to co-ordinate and carry out the plan. On the other hand, other professionals, especially those who did not have frequent contact with the health board, were critical of the lack of feedback they received from case conferences on the outcome of the recommendations.

FACTORS AFFECTING THE ONGOING MANAGEMENT OF CASES

In addition to constructive inter-agency and inter-professional co-operation, a number of other factors were identified by social workers as affecting the ongoing management of child abuse and neglect cases. Good supervision was the most important of those. Most workers were satisfied with the level of *informal* support and supervision they received from their managers. However, they considered the level of *formal* supervision to be, on the whole, limited and inadequate. While again emphasising the value of informal and personal support for workers, an important finding from this research was the need for their supervisors to complement this with regular formal supervision, where workers would have the opportunity to reflect on their complex work and consider issues other than the day-to-day management of individual cases.

STRUCTURAL SUPPORTS

Lack of basic structural social supports was another key factor which often impeded workers carrying out their work effectively. These included lack of office space for interviewing clients, limited access to office accommodation in rural regions of the health board, absence of security for staff in many of the offices (by way of reception personnel or security systems) and a lack of support for workers when carrying out home visits in isolated areas. Indicative of this was the number of workers who had experienced threats, either physical or verbal, or who feared such personal threats in the course of their work. In light of the stressful nature of child protection work itself, it was considered crucial that such issues were addressed within the Health Board. The final key factor appearing to affect the success with which workers could carry out their child protection duties was the size of their caseloads. The majority of social workers reported that they were unable to offer as complete a service as was required in the cases analysed, given the pressures of their other work.

PARENTAL INVOLVEMENT

In light of the *Child Care Act, 1991* and the recommendations of the Kilkenny Incest Inquiry (1993), the issue of parental involvement in the child protection process was a pertinent concern of the research. It was found that participation of parents, particularly at the initial stages of intervention, was found to be limited, despite a commitment to working in partnership with parents expressed in their local procedures, and a verbal aspiration towards increased participation reflected in interviews with most professionals. While most parents had been seen following the notification of alleged child abuse or neglect and were aware of at least some aspects of the initial child protection plans made, there was limited participation of parents in the actual construction of the intervention plans. None of the parents had attended a full case conference and in only three cases had a parent attended for some form of feedback at the end of the meetings.

In our interviews with the various professionals, including social workers, the notion of parental involvement in case conferences was generally supported. However, only one practitioner supported the notion of *full* participation of parents. Attendance by parents for some of the discussion or for feed-back were the preferred options by most professionals. In contrast, all but one of the parents expressed the desire to attend the whole case conference on their family, despite their acute awareness of the possible distress that could be caused by hearing their personal and family details being discussed. In general, parents wished not only to hear what was being said, but also felt they had a significant contribution to make to such meetings. Furthermore, the parents who did attend for just feedback from the case conference found the process humiliating, difficult and uncomfortable. Findings from the interviews with both professionals and parents highlight the desirability of a real commitment within the service to partnership with parents. The anxieties of professionals about full participation and the parents' experience of limited attendance also emphasises the challenge inherent in such an approach, the possible conflicts of interest which may exist between the participants, and the need to rethink the whole structure of the case conference process to enable real and meaningful participation for all members. Training and preparation of professionals, as well as parents, is essential before such an ideal can be achieved.[2]

Interviews with parents generated a number of other significant findings in relation to the way in which they viewed the intervention of the Health Board and the service which was offered to them following investigation. Of the parents who had been the alleged perpetrators, or partners of the perpetrators of abuse or neglect (half of the respondents), some were reasonably satisfied with the investigative process, while others were extremely upset and distressed by the intervention. Feelings of embarrassment, resentfulness, anger and traumatisation were most commonly reported. The parents whose children had been abused by a perpetrator outside the family, or by ex-partners, were less hostile to the investigation, and, in certain cases, found the intervention helpful where it resulted in a confirmation of their own suspicions or an offer of help to the family.

While many of the parents found the investigative process difficult, and resented the Health Board's involvement, the majority of parents interviewed acknowledged that they had developed generally positive relationships with their social workers, al-

---

[2] Initiatives such as the recent guide to parental participation in case conferences provided by the Southern Health Board (Gilligan and Chapman, 1997) are an example of possible steps which can be made in this regard.

though some expressed a lack of trust in the service. Most parents considered their children to have made progress since the initial investigation and were generally satisfied with the services their children had been offered. However, most parents were critical of the level of support or service they themselves had received from the social work service or elsewhere. The majority of parents perceived the South Eastern Health Board social work service as a service only for children, and even more narrowly, for children who had been alleged abused or neglected. Many of the parents interviewed reported that they were suffering from stress and depression, and many associated this directly with the current events relating to the child abuse allegations. Most parents voiced a need for counselling themselves and for services targeted at the family *as a whole* rather than only for the 'abused' child.

Findings from interviews with parents highlight their relatively powerless position within the child protection system in terms of their limited involvement in decision making in relation to their own families and their perception that the social work service was involved to offer help and support to the children, as opposed to themselves or to the family as a whole. A striking finding in this regard is that, despite the level of discomfort many felt with involvement of the social work service, the majority expressed a commitment to working with the service and a desire to be more actively involved in this. Parents were, on the whole, realistic about what the service could offer, and identified the kinds of services they considered most essential to enabling families such as their own.

DISCUSSION

One of the key findings of this research was that those families who were at the centre of concern regarding child abuse and neglect were predominantly drawn from the lower end of the social hierarchy. Such findings have been replicated elsewhere, but a satisfactory explanation for why this appears to be the case has yet to be fully articulated. Frost (1990) suggests that this is the case because such families are less able to measure up to the norms of family and domestic responsibility and are subject to greater surveillance by agents of the State, welfare officers, social workers, etc. Pelton (1978) suggests that child abuse is correlated with low socio-economic status and highlights what he terms the 'myth of classlessness' in child abuse. In other words, research evidence would suggest that child abuse is not distributed equally between the social classes, but is primarily to be found in families where financial problems exist; the parent(s) are considered to have immature personalities; where the mother lives with a male partner who is unemployed and not the biological father of the children. Yet if this is the case, and the research in the South Eastern Health Board largely confirmed the above stereo-type abusing family, Rodgers (1996) asks why have individualistic psychopathological explanations remained in the ascendancy. If child abuse is correlated strongly with financial and other indicators of deprivation, why does the 'myth of classlessness' represented by a clinical discourse rooted in the correction of behaviour deemed to be psychopathological persist?

A sociological discourse anchored in the social policy analysis of poverty would appear to offer more successful solutions to protect children, if the causes of child abuse are located in the poverty of families. Thus, we appear to have a contradiction between the observable distribution of child abuse in the class structure and how it is responded to. If poverty is the single most important determinant of child abuse, what role can community care social workers (the primary professional group identified in the study for investigating and managing child abuse) and other agents, i.e. Gardaí, psychologists, teachers, etc., play in protecting children? They are not in a position to alleviate poverty in families, provide good quality accommodation or create employment. Inter-agency and inter-professional collaboration may have a limited role in achieving some of these objectives, but only if a sufficient stock of low-cost good quality accommodation exists, if genuine employment and training opportunities exist, and if the risk of poverty decreases. It has been suggested that the reason why psychopathological explanations dominate our interpretation of the reason for child abuse is that such explanations facilitate a narrow clinical or medical response rather than a social policy response to child abuse. Rodgers argues that:

> . . . [t]o enclose the debate about child abuse and neglect
> within the parameters of a medical discourse means that
> relatively cheap strategies involving professional interven-
> tion and family therapy can be employed, relieving govern-
> ments of the need to address fundamental problems of the
> reward structure in advanced industrial economies. The
> advantage of this for policy makers within governmental
> circles is that the blame for failures in child protection can
> be contained to the level of negligent professional practice
> rather than being attributed to insufficient resources and
> poor social policy direction from the political centre (1996:
> 170).

The research in the South Eastern Health Board does not allow
us to satisfactorily explain why the majority of child abuse and
neglect referrals to the social work service came primarily from
families at the lower end of the social hierarchy. However, the response of the State in attempting to protect children from abuse
and neglect needs to be questioned. Are the development of for-
malised guidelines for the management of child abuse and neglect
cases and greater inter-agency and inter-professional collaboration the most appropriate way to advance the protection of children? Or are such developments further confirmation of the narrow lens through which responses to child abuse are viewed? Are
they simply a quasi-legal response to the management, rather
than the prevention, of child abuse and neglect? The evidence in
this research would suggest that there exists a social causation
and social pattern to child abuse. Yet the response of the child
welfare experts is to increase the surveillance mechanisms that
allow for the identification of 'dangerous families' (Parton & Parton, 1989). This perspective suggests that child abuse is distributed equally, if randomly, throughout the social structure and is a
result of defects in the character structure (Kempe *et al.*, 1962) or
other psychological problems. Essentially, it denies a *social* causation and concentrates on *individual* causation. Our research
does not offer a solution to these perplexing and contentious issues, rather it confirms a pattern evident elsewhere.

Our research does not suggest that child abuse is to be found
solely in the lower end of the social hierarchy, rather that state
intervention in a variety of guises is more prevalent for families

in this social position and thus various forms of child abuse are more easily identifiable. However, this does not explain why, in order to protect children in Ireland, the psychopathological and quasi-legal discourse remains dominant and the sociological discourse marginal. The micro-level analysis of the operation and perceptions of actors in the child protection system in one health board region in Ireland, in the context of the broader changes occurring nationally, as described in Chapter One, suggests that the concept of providing for the welfare of children is being replaced by a narrower concern with the protection of *certain* children from their dangerous families. This has been propelled by a number of public inquiries, which, by their nature, have been driven by the objective of ascertaining the 'facts' of the situation within a legalistic discourse. Likewise, new quasi-legal guidelines for community care social workers and other agencies lay stress on the management and allocation of agency responsibility for child protection.

Finally, the research suggests that the child welfare apparatus, in general, continues to be primarily child protection focused in its approach. The over-all system, as it is currently constructed, tends to frame its response to referrals within the context of the machinery of child protection; the 'investigation', the 'notification', 'child protection case conferences' and the use of specialist 'child abuse validation' units. Within this framework, assessments and interventions appear to be made more in the context of 'dangerousness' rather than 'need'. This research has shown that families often perceive this approach as stigmatising and neglectful of the more fundamental problems which may exist within the family. Other research has recommended that it would be more appropriate to re-frame the approach of the service in terms of 'need' rather than 'risk'. Gibbons, Conroy and Bell (1995), in relation to the UK situation, argue for the replacement of terms such as 'emotional abuse' and 'neglect' in official policy documents with the concept of 'in need', suggesting that referrals in the 'in need' category receive the same level of response as physical and sexual abuse allegations. From our research, a step further than this seems necessary. Allegations of child abuse and neglect must continue to receive an immediate response, but such problems should be framed within the broader ambit of 'families in need', where other crucial categories of family and individual difficulties, which are likely to feature also in child abuse and neglect cases, are considered in the serious manner they deserve, and offered a similarly comprehensive response from a community social work service. In line with the fundamental underpinnings of the *Child Care Act, 1991*, resources for preventative services should be aimed at addressing the needs of the welfare of children and their families within the community who are experiencing a range of problems, of which child abuse and neglect issues should be a crucial, but not exclusive, concern.

The challenge for the future is the need to embrace a plurality of perspectives on both the prevention of, and response to, child abuse and neglect in Ireland. Such a development would challenge and confront our existing preconceptions of child abuse and neglect and open up a conceptual and political space that would move us away from the narrow discourse that has dominated the debate in Ireland to date.

BIBLIOGRAPHY

Barnes, J. (1989) *Irish Industrial Schools 1868–1908*. Dublin: Irish Academic Press.

Borough of Brent, London (1985) *A Child in Trust*. (The Beckford Report) The report of the panel of inquiry into the death of Jasmine Beckford. London: London Borough of Brent.

Breen, R., Hannan, D., Rottman, D., Whelan, T. (1990) *Understanding Contemporary Ireland: State, Class and Development in the Republic of Ireland*. Dublin: Gill and Macmillan.

Buckley, H. (1996) 'Child abuse guidelines in Ireland: for whose protection?' in H. Ferguson and T. McNamara (eds.) *Protecting Irish Children: Investigation, Protection and Welfare*, special edition of *Administration*, Vol. 44, No. 2, pp. 37–56.

Buckley, H. (1993) 'The Kilkenny Incest Investigation: some practice implications'. *Irish Social Worker*, Vol. 11, No. 4, pp. 6–7.

Buckley, H. (1996) *Beyond the Rhetoric: A Qualitative Study of Child Protection in Ireland*. Paper presented to the ISPCAN Congress, Dublin, August 1996.

Burke, H. (1987) *The People and The Poor Law in 19th Century Ireland*. Dublin: Web Press.

Butler, S. (1996) 'Child protection or professional self-preservation by the baby nurses? Public health nurses and child protection in Ireland'. *Social Science and Medicine*, Vol. 43, No. 3, pp. 303–314.

Butler-Sloss, Lord Justice E. (1988) *Report of the Inquiry into Child Abuse in Cleveland in 1987*. London: HMSO.

CARE Memorandum (1972) *Children Deprived*. Dublin.

Carlile Inquiry (1987) *A Child in Mind: Protection of Children in a Responsible Society*. The Report of the Commission of Inquiry into the circumstances surrounding the death of Kimberly Carlile. London: London Borough of Greenwich.

Central Statistics Office (1994) *Census '91*. Dublin: Government Publications Office.

Central Statistics Office (1996) *Labour Force Survey 1995*. Dublin: Government Publications Office.

Cheetham, J., Fuller, R., McIvor, G., and Petch, A. (1992) *Evaluating Social Work Effectiveness*. London: Open University Press.

Clear, C. (1987) *Nuns in Nineteenth Century Ireland*. Dublin: Gill and Macmillan.

Cleaver, H. and Freeman, P. (1995) *Parental Perspectives in Cases of Suspected Child Abuse*. London: HMSO.

Colwell Report (1974) *Report of the Committee of Inquiry into the Care and Supervision Provided in Relation to Maria Colwell*. London: HMSO.

Commission of Inquiry into the Reformatory and Industrial School System (1936) *Report*. Dublin: Stationery Office.

Cooney, T. and Torode, R. (1989) *Irish Council for Civil Liberties Working Party on Child Sexual Abuse Report*. Dublin: ICCL.

Corby, B. (1987) *Working with Child Abuse*. Milton Keynes: Open University Press.

Corby, B., Millar, M. and Young, L. (1996) 'Parental participation in child protection work: Rethinking the rhetoric'. *British Journal of Social Work*, Vol. 26, No. 4, pp. 475–492.

Council for Social Welfare (1972) *Child Care*. Dublin: Council for Social Welfare.

Cousins, M. (1996) *Seen and Heard: Promoting and Protecting Children's Rights in Ireland*. The Children's Rights Alliance — Republic of Ireland.

Department of Education (1928) *Report of the Department of Education for the School Years 1925–26–27 and the Financial and Administrative Year 1926–27*. Dublin: Stationery Office.

Department of Education (1991) *Procedures for Dealing with Allegations or Suspicions of Child Abuse*. Dublin: Department of Education.

Department of Education (1994) *School Attendance/Truancy Report*. Dublin: Department of Education.

Department of Foreign Affairs (1996) *UN Convention on the Rights of the Child — First National Report for Ireland*. Dublin: Stationery Office.

Department of Health (1973) *Guidelines for Development of Social Work Services (In Community Care Programme)*. Dublin: Department of Health.

Department of Health (1976) *Report of Committee on Non-Accidental Injury to Children*. Dublin: Stationery Office.

Department of Health (1977) *Memorandum on Non Accidental Injury to Children*. Dublin: Stationery Office.

Department of Health (1980) *Non-Accidental Injury to Children. Guidelines on Procedures for the Identification, Investigation and Management of Non-Accidental Injury to Children*. Dublin: Department of Health.

Department of Health (1980) *Task Force on Child Care Services: Final Report*. Dublin: Stationery Office.

Department of Health (1983) *Non-Accidental Injury to Children: Guidelines on Procedures for the Identification, Investigation and Management of Non-Accidental Injury to Children*. Dublin: Department of Health.

Department of Health (1987) *Child Abuse Guidelines: Guidelines on Procedures for the Identification, Investigation and Management of Child Abuse*. Dublin: Department of Health.

Department of Health (1994) *Shaping a Healthier Future*. Dublin: Government Publications Office.

Department of Health (1995a) *Child Abuse Statistics 1987–1994*. Dublin: Department of Health.

Department of Health (1995b) *Notification of Suspected Cases of Child Abuse between the Health Boards and the Gardaí*. Dublin: Department of Health.

Department of Health (1996) *Putting Children First: a Discussion Document on Mandatory Reporting of Child Abuse*. Dublin: Department of Health.

Department of Health (1996) *Report on the Inquiry into the Operation of Madonna House*. Dublin: Stationery Office.

Department of Health. *Survey of Children In Care of Health Boards. Various Years*. Dublin: Child Care Division, Department of Health.

Department of Health (UK) (1991) *Working Together Under the Children Act 1989*. London: HMSO.

Dingwall, R. (1989) 'Labelling children as abused or neglected'. In: W. Stainton Rogers, Hevey, D. and Ash, E. (eds.) *Child Abuse and Neglect: Facing the Challenge*. London: Batsford.

Dingwall, R., Eekelaar, J. and Murray, T. (1983) *The Protection of Children: State Intervention and Family Life*. Oxford: Blackwell.

Doherty, D. (1996) 'Child care and protection: Protecting the children — supporting their service providers'. *Administration*, Vol. 44, No. 2, pp. 102–113.

Fahey, T. (1992) 'State, family and compulsory schooling in Ireland'. *Economic and Social Review*, Vol. 23, No. 4, pp. 369–395.

Farmer, E. and Owen, M. (1995) *Child Protection Practice: Private Risks and Public Remedies*. London: HMSO.

Ferguson, H. (1993) 'Surviving Irish childhood: child protection and the death of children in child abuse cases in Ireland since 1884'. In: H. Ferguson, R. Gilligan, R. Torode (eds.) *Surviving Childhood Adversity: Issues for Policy and Practice*. Dublin: Social Studies Press.

Ferguson, H. (1994) 'Child abuse inquiries and the Report of the Kilkenny Incest Investigation: a critical analysis'. *Administration*, Vol. 41, No. 4, pp. 385–410.

Ferguson, H. (1995) 'Child welfare, child protection and the *Child Care Act 1991*: Key issues for policy and practice'. In: H. Ferguson and P. Kenny (eds.) *On Behalf of The Child: Child Welfare, Child Protection and The Child Care Act 1991*. Dublin: A & A Farmar.

Ferguson, H. (1996) 'Protecting Irish children in time: Child abuse as a social problem and the development of the child protection system in the Republic of Ireland' in H. Ferguson and T. McNamara (eds.) *Protecting Irish Children: Investigation, Protection and Welfare*, special edition of *Administration*, Vol. 44, No. 2, pp. 5–36.

Ferguson, H. and Kenny, P. (1995) *On Behalf of the Child: Child Welfare, Child Protection and the Child Care Act, 1991*. Dublin: A & A Farmar.

Ferguson, H., Gilligan, R., Torode R. (eds.) (1993) *Surviving Childhood Adversity: Issues for Policy and Practice*. Dublin: Social Studies Press.

Frost, N. (1990) 'Official intervention and child protection: The relationship between state and family in contemporary Britain'. In The Violence Against Children Study Group, *Taking Child Abuse Seriously*. London: Routledge.

Gibbons, J., Conroy, S. and Bell, C. (1995) *Operating the Child Protection System: A Study of Child Protection Practices in English Local Authorities*. London: HMSO.

Gilligan, R. (1989) Policy in the Republic of Ireland: Historical and current issues. In: P. Carter, T. Jeffs and M. Smith (eds.) *Social Work and Social Welfare Yearbook*. Milton Keynes: Open University.

Gilligan, R. (1991) *Irish Child Care Services: Policy, Practice and Provision*. Dublin: Institute of Public Administration.

Gilligan, R. (1992) *The Future Role of the Church in Child Care — A Discussion Paper*. Prepared for the Conference of Major Religious Superiors, The Catholic Social Service Conference, and the Sacred Heart Home Trust.

Gilligan, R. (1992–93) 'The *Child Care Act 1991*: An examination of its scope and resource implications'. *Administration*, Vol. 40, No. 4, pp. 347–370.

Gilligan, R. (1993) 'Ireland'. In: M.J. Colton and W. Hellinckx (eds.) *Child Care in EC: A Country-specific Guide to Foster and Residential Care*. Aldershot: Arena.

Gilligan, R. (1996) 'Irish child care services in the 1990s: The Child Care Act 1991 and other developments'. In: M. Hill and J. Aldgate (eds.) *Child Welfare Services: Developments in Law, Policy, Practice and Research*. London: Jessica Kingsley Publishers.

Gilligan, R. and Chapman, R. (1997) *Developing Good Practice in the Conduct of Child Protection Case Conferences — An Action-Research Project*. Cork: Southern Health Board.

Greene, D. (1979) 'Legal aspects of non-accidental injury to children'. *Administration*, Vol. 27. No. 4, pp. 460–474.

Hallett, C. (1995a) *Inter-Agency Co-operation in Child Protection*. London: HMSO.

Hallett, C. (1995b) *Working Together in Child Protection*. London: HMSO.

Hallett, C. and Birchall, E. (1992) *Co-ordination and Child Protection: A Review of the Literature*. Edinburgh: HMSO.

Hallett, C. and Stevenson, O. (1980) *Child Abuse: Aspects of Interprofessional Co-operation*. London: George Allen & Unwin.

Hancock, W.N. (1859) 'On the importance of substituting the family system of rearing orphan children for the system now pursued in our workhouses'. *Journal of the Statistical and Social Inquiry Society of Ireland*, Vol. 2.

Hooper, C.A. (1992) *Mothers Surviving Child Sexual Abuse*. London: Routledge.

Howe, D. (1996) 'Surface and depth in social work practice'. In: *Social Theory, Social Change and Social Work*. London: Routledge.

Irish Association of Social Workers (1976) *Comments on the Report of the Committee on Non Accidental Injury to Children*. Dublin: IASW.

Irish Catholic Bishops Advisory Committee on Child Sexual Abuse by Priests and Religious (1996) *Child Sexual Abuse: Framework for a Church*. Dublin: Veritas.

Johnson, Z. and Molloy, B. (1995) 'The Community Mothers Programme: empowerment of parents by parents'. *Children and Society*, Vol. 9, No. 2, pp. 73–85.

Keenan, O. (1996) *Kelly — A Child is Dead*. Interim Report of the Joint Committee on the Family. Dublin: Government Publications Office.

Kempe, C.H., Silverman, F.N., Steel, B.F., Drogemueller, W. and Silver, H.K. (1962) 'The battered child syndrome'. *Journal of the American Medical Association*, 181, pp. 17–24.

Kempe, H. and Helfer, R. (1968) *The Battered Child*. Chicago: University of Chicago Press.

Kenny, P. (1995) 'The Child Care Act 1991 and the social context of child protection'. In H. Ferguson and P. Kenny (eds.) *On Behalf of the Child: Child Welfare, Child Protection and the Child Care Act 1991*. Dublin: A & A Farmar.

Killion, M. (1993) 'Dilemmas in dealing with domestic violence'. *Irish Social Worker*, Vol. 11, No. 3, p. 11.

Law Reform Commission (1990) *Report on Child Sexual Abuse*. Dublin: Law Reform Commission.

Luddy, M. (1995) *Women and Philanthropy in Nineteenth-Century Ireland*. Cambridge: Cambridge University Press.

Maguire, C. (1996) 'The living Constitution: Managing the unruly child'. *Irish Law Times*, Vol. 14, pp. 63–66.

McCashin, A. (1996) *Lone Mothers in Ireland: A Local Study*. Combat Poverty Agency Research Report Series. Dublin: Oak Tree Press.

McGrath, K. (1996) 'Intervening in child sexual abuse in Ireland: Towards victim centred policies and practices'. *Administration,* Vol. 44, No. 2; pp. 57–72.

McGuinness, C. (1993) *Report of The Kilkenny Incest Investigation.* Dublin: Stationery Office.

McKeown, K. and Gilligan, R. (1991) 'Child sexual abuse in the Eastern Health Board region of Ireland in 1988: An analysis of 512 confirmed cases'. *The Economic and Social Review,* Vol. 22, No. 2, pp. 101–134.

Merrick, D. (1996) *Social Work and Child Abuse.* London: Routledge.

Milner, J. (1993) Avoiding violent men: The gendered nature of child protection policy and practice'. In: H. Ferguson, R. Gilligan and R. Torode (eds.) *Surviving Childhood Adversity: Issues for Policy and Practice.* Dublin: Social Studies Press.

Murphy, M. (1996) 'From prevention to "Family Support" and beyond: Promoting the welfare of Irish children'. *Administration,* Vol. 44, No. 2, pp. 73–101.

NESC (1987) *Community Care Services: An Overview.* Dublin: National Economic and Social Council.

NESC (1996) *Strategy into the 21st Century.* Dublin: National Economic and Social Council.

O'Connor, P. (1992) 'Child care policy: A provocative analysis and research agenda'. *Administration,* Vol. 40, No. 3, pp. 200–219.

O'Doherty, C. (1996) 'The functioning of child care advisory committees — is partnership possible?' *Irish Social Worker,* Vol. 14, No. 1, pp. 11–13.

O'Sullivan, D. (1979) 'Social definition in child care in the Irish Republic: Models of child and child care intervention'. *Economic and Social Review,* Vol. 10, No. 3, April, pp. 209–230.

O'Sullivan, E. (1993) 'Irish Child Care Law — The origins, aims and development of the *1991 Child Care Act*'. *Childright* (June) No. 93.

O'Sullivan, E. (1995) 'Section 5 of the *Child Care Act, 1991* and youth homelessness', pp. 84–104. In: H. Ferguson and P. Kenny (eds.) *On Behalf of the Child: Child Welfare, Child Protection and the Child Care Act, 1991.* A & A Farmer Press.

O'Sullivan, E. (1996a) 'Adolescents leaving care, leaving home and child care provision in Ireland and the UK: A critical view'. In: M. Hill and J. Aldgate (eds.) *Child Welfare Services: Developments in Law, Policy, Practice and Research.* Jessica Kingsley Publishers.

O'Sullivan, E. (1996b) 'Juvenile justice in the Republic of Ireland — future priorities'. *Irish Social Worker*, Vol. 14, No. 2/4. pp. 4–7.

Opgenhaffen, R. (1996) *The Family — Family Support Worker Relationship — A Study of Five Cases Based on Perceptions of the Family, Family Support Worker and Social Worker*. M. Sc. Thesis, Department of Social Studies, Trinity College, Dublin.

Parton, C. and Parton, N. (1989) 'Child abuse, the Law and dangerousness'. In O. Stevenson (ed.) *Child Abuse: Public Policy and Professional Practice*. Hemel Hempstead: Harvester Wheatsheaf.

Parton, N. (1991) *Governing the Family: Child Care, Child Protection and the State*. Basingstoke: Macmillan.

Parton, N. (1996) 'Social work, risk and the blaming system'. In: N. Parton (ed.) *Social Theory, Social Change and Social Work*. London: Routledge.

Pelton, L. (1978) 'Child abuse and neglect: The myth of classlessness'. *American Journal of Orthopsychiatry*, Vol. 48, No. 4, pp. 608–17.

Pithouse, A. (1987) *Social Work: The Social Organisation of an Invisible Trade*. Aldershot: Gower Publishing.

Reder, P., Duncan, S. and Gray, M. (1993) *Beyond Blame: Child Abuse Tragedies Revisited*. London: Routledge.

Report on Industrial Schools and Reformatories (The Kennedy Report) (1970) Dublin: The Stationery Office.

Robins, J. (1980) *The Lost Children: A Study of Charity Children in Ireland 1700–1900*. Dublin: Institute of Public Administration.

Rodgers, J. (1996) *Family Life and Social Control: A Sociological Perspective*. Basingstoke: Macmillan.

Senior Social Workers, Eastern Health Board (1976) *Report of Committee on Non Accidental Injury to Children — Senior Social Workers' Comments*. Policy document issued by the Eastern Health Board Senior Social Workers.

Skehill, C. (1997) *Exploring the Nature of Social Work: An Historical Perspective*. Occasional Paper Series, Trinity College, Dublin.

Smith, S. and Deasy, P. (1977) 'Child abuse in Ireland'. *The Journal of the Irish Medical Association*, Vol. 70, No. 3, pp. 65–79.

South Eastern Health Board (1994) *Report on the Adequacy of Child Care and Family Support Services for 1993*. South Eastern Health Board.

South Eastern Health Board (1995) *Report on the Adequacy of Child Care and Family Support Services for 1994*. South Eastern Health Board.

South Eastern Health Board (1996) *Report on the Adequacy of Child Care and Family Support Services for 1995*. South Eastern Health Board.

Thoburn, J., Lewis, A. and Shemmings, D. (1995) *Paternalism or Partnership? Family Involvement in the Child Protection Process.* London: HMSO.

Thorpe, D. (1994) *Evaluating Child Protection*. Milton Keynes: Open University Press.

Tuairim. (1966) *Some of our Children — A Report on the Residential Care of the Deprived Child in Ireland.* Tuairim: London.

Waterhouse, L. and Carnie, J. (1990) 'Investigating child sexual abuse: towards inter-agency co-operation'. *Adoption and Fostering*, Vol. 14., No. 4., pp. 7–12.